I0117471

John James Edmonstoune Linton

A Prohibitory Liquor Law for Upper Canada

A Bill for an Act to Prohibit the Sale by Retail

John James Edmonstoune Linton

A Prohibitory Liquor Law for Upper Canada
A Bill for an Act to Prohibit the Sale by Retail

ISBN/EAN: 9783743423565

Manufactured in Europe, USA, Canada, Australia, Japa

Cover: Foto ©Suzi / pixelio.de

Manufactured and distributed by brebook publishing software
(www.brebook.com)

John James Edmonstoune Linton

A Prohibitory Liquor Law for Upper Canada

A PROHIBITORY LIQUOR LAW

FOR UPPER CANADA,

BEING

A BILL

FOR AN ACT TO PROHIBIT THE SALE BY RETAIL, &c.,

WITH REMARKS, AND OTHER DOCUMENTS.

BY J. J. E. LINTON,

(CLERK PEACE CO. PERTH.)

" Have they not got enough of our blood."—Hon. M. Cameron.

WITH PORTRAIT OF HON. M. CAMERON, M.P.P.

TORONTO:

PRINTED BY MACLEAR & CO., KING STREET.

1860.

The "Challenge," a Temperance Periodical, is published occasionally by J. J. E. Linton, Stratford, C. W. The first number was issued April, 1854.

STRATFORD, C. W., *6th February*, 1860.

HON. MALCOLM CAMERON, M.P.P.,

DEAR SIR,

Permit me as a small token of friendship, and also of approval of your efforts in the cause of Temperance and Prohibition, to inscribe the following sheets to you. I hope that you will long be preserved to advocate the interests of Canada for its progress in " social advantages :" which in all countries should, I think, have some weight and consideration with legislators, who are entrusted with the fullest powers to consider what are the best measures for the *public good.*

I am, dear Sir,

Yours sincerely,

J. J. E. LINTON.

CONTENTS.

PROHIBITION OF RETAIL OF LIQUORS.

[CIRCULAR.]

STRATFORD, C.W., *6th February*, 1860.

SIR,

I crave your help and assistance to promote the passing, in Provincial Parliament, a law the same as, or similar to, the subjoined Bill.

On an inspection of the bill, it will at once be seen that it deals only with the trade or traffic in Intoxicating Liquors, so far only as *the Retail* is concerned. The present laws of the Province as to the manufacture, importation and exportation, and the wholesale of said liquors, are not touched. The writer considers—others consider—and he hopes to have shewn by the subjoined papers, that *the evils*, as the results which flow from the trade and traffic, are connected with the *retail*; so much so, as to induce an expectation that *that portion*, at least, of the trade will be legislated upon and restrained — excepting for medicinal, chemical, mechanical, and sacramental purposes.

Having this hope— and also retrospectively considering the measure as to the restraint on the sale of liquors, from Saturday night till Monday morning, which twelve months ago I laid before the public, and which was ultimately, with improved amendments, passed by the Legislature on 26th March last, the Act 22 Vic. cap. 6,—having this hope, the writer expects that petitions in favor of the subjoined bill will be prepared and presented to Parliament. A form of petition to both Houses of Parliament is subjoined.

Your very obedient Servant,

J. J. E. LINTON,
Clerk of the Peace, Co. of Perth.

To the Legislative Assembly of the Province of Canada.

The Petition of the undersigned, Inhabitants of ———

Humbly sheweth,—That your petitioners crave your Honourable House to pass and sanction a measure, as a law of this Upper Province, for a Prohibition and restraint on the retail sale and traffic in Intoxicating drinks, except for medicinal, chemical, mechanical, and sacramental purposes. And your Petitioners will ever pray.

Dated at ———

————

To the Honourable the Legislative Council of the Province of Canada.

The Petition of the undersigned, Inhabitants of ———

Humbly sheweth,—That your petitioners crave your Honourable House to pass and sanction a measure, as a law of this Upper Province, for a Prohibition and restraint on the retail sale and traffic in Intoxicating drinks, except for medicinal, chemical, mechanical, and sacramental purposes. And your petitioners will ever pray.

Dated at———

PROHIBITORY BILL.

An Act to Prohibit the Sale by Retail of Spirituous and Fermented Liquors, within that part of the Province called Upper Canada.

WHEREAS it is provided by Section 245, Sub-section 6, of the Act passed in the twenty-second year of Her Majesty's reign, chapter ninety-nine, intituled *An Act respecting the Municipal Institutions of Upper Canada*, that the sale by retail of sprituous and fermented liquors in any Inn or other house of public entertainment, and in shops and places other than houses of public entertainment, in every Township, City, Town and Incorporated Village in Upper Canada, may by a By-Law, be prohibited, provided before the final passing of such By-Law the same has been duly approved by the Electors of the Municipality; and whereas it has been found inconvenient and of doubtful accomplishment for universal purposes, the passing of such By-Laws,—Therefore, Her Majesty, by and with the advice and consent of the Legislative Council and Assembly of Canada, enacts as follows:—

1. That within the limits of each Municipality of every Township, Incorporated Village, Town and City in Upper Canada, there shall not be (excepting as in this Act excepted) from and after the passing of this act, any sale by retail of any spirituous or fermented Liquors, in any Inn or other house of public entertainment, or in any shop or place, other than houses of public entertainment; *Provided* hereby, that any sale by retail of said Liquors, not herein in this Act excepted and provided for, shall be illegal, and shall be punishable, as hereinafter enacted:—

2. That there shall be saved and excepted from the operation of the preceding section, the rights and privileges by the licenses which are or may be issued on behalf of each of the said Municipalities, until the expiry of the period for which these licenses respectively were issued,—and also there shall be saved and excepted as said is, the sale of said liquors, as herein in the next section of this Act provided for, for medicinal, chemical and mechanical, or wine for sacramental purposes,—and for such purposes the order, certificate or requisition, signed by a licensed medical practitioner, or sig. ed by the Mayor, or a Justice of the Peace of any City or Town, or by a Justice of the Peace of the County wherein either of the aforesaid Municipalities shall be, or by a Reeve, or Deputy Reeve in such County, or by any three rate-payers of either of said Municipalities wherein the vendor after mentioned shall be licensed, or in the case of sacramental purposes, an order, certificate, or requisition, signed by the clergyman of the church, meeting house, or place of worship, where the same may be required, shall be required to be produced and delivered by the vendee or his agent to the licensed vender or his agent.

3. That for the purpose of providing for the sale by retail of said liquors for the aforesaid purposes, each of the said Municipalities by the respective councils thereof, shall have the power, and they are hereby authorised to grant a license or licenses available within the limits of each of their said Municipalities, to any person or persons, he or they being freeholders in the County where such license is granted, (who may be known as the licensed vender or venders,) for the sale by retail of said liquors for the aforesaid purposes; provided hereby that there shall only be one such license, and one place for the sale by retail of said liquors, for any number of inhabitants in any municipality, not exceeding two thousand, and for every two thousand inhabitants or part of two thousand inhabitants over and above the first two thousand, one license and one such place; each such license to be for one year, said year to end on the last day of February in each and every year; and for each of such licenses the said municipality shall be entitled to demand, and to receive, and to apply for corporation purposes as by

law provided, any sum not less than twenty-five dollars, nor more than eight hundred dollars, the same to be inclusive of the duty payable under the Imperial statute referred to in the Act cited in the preamble hereof, but exclusive of the sum payable to the Province, in conformity with the present laws thereof; and provided also that each of said Municipalities shall have power by By-Law to fix the amount payable for each such license in conformity with the provisions in this Act contained, and also to decide on the person or persons, he or they being freeholders in the County where such license is granted, to whom said license shall be given, and also shall have power by said By-Law to make restrictions or rules as to the character and standing of the said person or persons; but no act by either of said Municipalities to be done, shall be contrary to, and if so done contrary, shall not affect or annul the enactments and provisions of this Act.

4. That it shall be lawful for the said medicinal and sacramental purposes, to sell as said is the said liquors on any day; provided hereby, that said liquors or any of them allowed to be sold by this Act, shall not be used for drinking purposes as a beverage, nor shall they or any of them be consumed or drunk, on the place or premises of the vender or his agent where sold; and also provided, that such place or premises shall not be in, or attached to, any store or shop, saloon, eating-house, house of entertainment, inn, hotel, tavern, or place, where by law the said liquors now are, or hitherto have been allowed to be manufactured or sold.

5. That the said licensed vender or his agent, shall keep a book, and shall therein enter and record each sale made, and shall for each such sale enter and record the same by entering and recording in said boo'., the name of the vendee or his agent, the name or names signed to and the date of said order, certificate or requisition, the date of sale, the quantity sold, the kind or quality and name of said liquors so sold, the purpose for which the same is so sold, and the price or sum so paid by the vendee or his agent therefor, according as nearly as may be to the form set forth in schedule A to this Act subjoined; and shall also keep and retain the said order, certificate or requisition, for at least one month after the date of said entry; and any rate-payer of the municipality wherein said vender or his agent shall so sell, shall be entitled and have the right and privilege on any lawful day, during the hours of the ordinary business of said vender or his agent, to inspect said book and also the said order, certificate, or requisition, and to make therefrom any extracts, on paying to said vender or his agent for said inspection and making said extracts the sum of ten cents; and each one of the said licensed venders or his agent, shall on the first Monday of the month after he commences to sell, deposit a copy duly certified as "a true copy," of the entries in said book up to the date of said first Monday, and shall thereafter deposit on each succeeding first Monday of each succeeding month, for the time while said license continues, a copy duly certified as "a true copy," of the entries in said book, from the time when so previously made, up to the date of said last mentioned first Monday, with the clerk of the Municipality which granted said vender the license; and all sales made by said vender or his agent, shall be for cash and not on credit.

6. That any person or persons or body, who shall be found by himself, or herself, or themselves, or itself, or his, her, or their, or its, servants, agents, or tenants, to have contravened or violated at any time or place the first enactment and the provisions in the fourth enactment in this Act contained, or any part thereof, the same shall be considered as an offence against this Act, and shall pay for said offence a fine of not less than fifty dollars, with costs, in case of conviction, and the said fine and costs when not paid, shall be recoverable from and leviable against the goods and chattels of the person or persons convicted; and upon a certificate on oath by the constable or other legal officer, that there is no sufficient distress to be found and to be levied upon belonging to the person or persons so convicted, the said person or persons so convicted shall be im-

prisoned in the common gaol of the county wherein the said offence may have been made, for the space of one month, with hard labor, unless the said fine and costs and costs of imprisonment, be sooner paid,—and in the case of refusal or non-compliance, by the vender or his agent to keep said book, or to enter and record the said sales therein, or to deposit the copy or copies of the entries, or to allow the inspection or the extracts to be made, all as provided for in the fifth section of this Act, the person or persons so refusing or non-complying shall be considered as offending against this Act, and shall for each case of refusal or non-compliance, be liable to pay a fine of not less than twenty-dollars, to be prosecuted for, and to be recoverable, and imprisonment therefor for one month to be made in the same way and manner as is provided for in this section as to other offences and fines; and it is hereby enacted that convictions when made, shall not relieve the person or persons convicted, of the liability to be prosecuted for a misdemeanor under this Act, if amenable to be so prosecuted; and that convictions for several said offences against this Act, may be made under this Act although such several offences may have been committed in the same day.

7. Any person or persons may be the informant or informants, complainant or complainants, in prosecuting under this Act,—all proceedings shall be begun within twenty days from the date of the offence, all informations, complaints, or other necessary proceedings may be brought and heard before any one or more Justices of the Peace of the County, Mayor, or Police Magistrate, or Justice of the Peace of a town or city, Reeve, or Deputy Reeve, where the offence or offences were committed or done, and the mode of procedure in, and the forms appended to, the Act sixteenth Victoria, chapter one hundred and seventy-eight, for summary proceedings, may be followed as regards the cases and proceedings under this Act.

8. The said fines or any portion of them which may be recovered, shall be paid to the convicting Justice, Mayor, Police Magistrate, Reeve or Deputy Reeve, or other acting Justice in the case, and by him paid equally, one half to the informant or complainant, and the other half to the treasurer of the Municipality where the said offence or offences were committed or done.

9 The word "Liquors" in this Act mentioned, shall be understood to comprehend and mean all malt liquors, and all liquors and combinations of liquors, or drinks used as drinking beverages, which are intoxicating.

10. That any knowingly false pretence or false statements or representation done or made, and whether knowingly done or made in writing or verbally, by the vender or his agent, vendee or his agent, or by any person or persons, or body, or his, her, or their or its servants, agents or tenants, in and as respects the selling and buying, obtaining or procuring the liquors specified in this Act, and as allowed to be vended and sold as in this Act provided, shall be considered as a misdemeanor, and shall be dealt with according to law.

11. All provisions in any Acts relative to the sale by retail of said liquors in that part of the Province called Upper Canada, inconsistent with the provisions of this Act, are hereby repealed.

12. This Act shall apply to Upper Canada only.

SCHEDULE A.

Book kept by (name ————— ————— ,) a Vender Licensed within the Municipality of (name of Township, &c.) according to the Act (title and chapter of this Act).

Name of Vendee or Agent.	Name or names to the Order, &c.	Year and Date of Order, &c.	Year and Date of Sale.	Quantity Sold	Kind and name of Liquor sold.	For what purpose.	Price paid by Vendee or his Agent.	Remarks.
Peter Leitch....	W. Smith, (Reeve.)	1860, March 4.	1860, March 4.	1 Quart.	Whiskey.	Mechanical.	20 Cents.	
James Boyd.....	L. Watson, J. P....	" " 10.	" " 10.	1 Pint.	Madeira Wine.	Medicinal.	50 Cents.	
John Forbes....	Rev. T. Stevenson.	" April 15.	" April 15.	1 Gallon.	Port Wine.	Sacramental.	Four Dollars.	
W. Strowger.....	J. Hyde, M.D......	" May 6.	" May 6.	2 Gallons.	Gin.	Chemical.	Eight Dollars.	

NOTE.—The above Prohibitory Bill was published in the Canada Temperance *Advocate*, Montreal, February 1, 1860.

REMARKS FOR A PROHIBITORY LIQUOR LAW.

1. If our Legislators are in earnest to consider the great question, viz.—" What is *one of the best questions* to be considered by us, in " Parliament, for the social good of the people for whom we are here " assembled to legislate, and which question *we can*, as legislators if " united and agreed, carry by our votes "—if that " great question," as it is one, is seen to be the Retail Traffic in Intoxicating Drinks and its restriction and Prohibition, then why should any good man, a Member of Parliament, in the face of the God who created him, hesitate to vote for it?

2. When the Temperance movement was inaugurated in the United States, so many years ago, and was in 1829 carried across the Atlantic and first adopted and acted on, in that year, in Ireland; and in September, also in that year, as the writer of these remarks well knows,—was begun and also acted upon in Greenock, Scotland, by the Father of Temperance Societies in Great Britain, yet living, John Dunlop, Esq., of Greenock (brother of the late well known and generous hearted Dr. Dunlop of Canada) it was ushered before a British public *and sustained*, when only a very small portion of facts relative to the extent of the Liquor Traffic, and the enormities in " common life " which that Traffic caused, were known ;—shall it be said now, at this day, when facts upon facts, statistics upon statistics, histories and narrations of the dire and cruel evils which that traffic has caused in society are written, circulated and made public by the thousand and hundreds of thousands, in tracts, in periodicals, in volumes, and in every shape,—shall it be said now, in this free Province, one of the best appendages of the British Empire, in the face of these statements,—that there should be no restriction, no prohibition, of that Traffic?

3. It is to be hoped, for the sake of humanity, for the sake of our Christian religion, that there are few in our noble Province of Canada, who will publicly support that negative action.

4. It is to be hoped, that there is not at this moment to be found a Minister of Jesus Christ, *of any Church*, in this Province, who will publicly support that negative action.

5. If there is, unhappily for our civilized race, any one person to be found in this Province, who will *publicly* by statement or other mode in words, printed or spoken, support the Retail Traffic and trade in Intoxicating Drinks, as now exercised in our midst, and as one *not dangerous* to society, and as being innocuous or harmless like the sales of and dealings in fruit, flour, grain, sugar, &c.,—*let such beware.*

6. Take the history of *any one* of the forty two counties in Upper Canada,—and we know something of the history of a few of them in the west, and especially of Perth, Huron and Bruce, (in the country which forms the former of which we settled " amongst the trees" in July, 1838,)—take that history, as regards the effects of the retail

Liquor Traffic, on the social position of its inhabitants, *now while we write*, and for cinquennial periods of five years backwards, to the first settlement of each county, and what will that history reveal? It will reveal *in its connections*, a category of crimes, offences, miseries, destitutions and social vices, *which would appal the ideas and thoughts of any heathen people*, to whom we are so fond of sending missionaries to. That missionary spirit is very well as an "idea;" as "idea" it only appears, in the position we are in, or rather, as being nearer the truth, in the position we have placed and do place ourselves in.

7. Gigantic as have the strides been, in the midst of a civilized and a "religion professing" people, of this hateful traffic and trade in intoxicating drinks, it is nowhere to be found in such luxuriance, and with a seeming agreableness of culture, and with *a relish*, as it is to be found generally in the three "religion professing" orders and sections of Christ's church,—namely, the Presbyterian, Episcopalian, and Roman Catholic. This *distinctive* allocation of the traffic, and also of the drinkers and consumers, we have years by-gone pointed out :—though the statement seemed to *startle* some of the members of the Presbyterian Synod in June, 1859, particularly one reverend gentleman, when a memorial by the writer was presented, with a conviction list of offences, &c., extending over *six feet* in length, and being only for offences, &c., for ninety days in this county. The writer of these remarks does not, however, believe, that either the officiating ministers or priests or doctors of divinity, of these sections of Christ's church, *believe*, or that the members or adherents of these churches in their inmost thoughts *believe*, that the glory of God, the advancement of Christianity, the humanization and civilization of our common race,—white, black, copper-colored or of any colour,—will be advanced and forwarded by the sales by retail, and by the various modes of *the public drinking*, of Brandy, Gin, Rum, Whiskey, Wines, (the latter composed of Sherry, Port, Madeira, Champagne, &c.,) or by Ales, Porter, &c.,*—or that they all and each *believe* that the divine author of all created things, the God whom they recognize and are so forward in public to worship, will delight or smile upon *the effects* of the above traffic or trade, or on the trade itself.—If it is so, then, *what is the belief*, as exercised in these three churches ?

8. The writer of these remarks, being a Presbyterian, would beg, humbly, to submit to be investigated the very important question : Is it the fact, or is it not, that in the importation, exportation, and in the manufacture, and the wholesale and the retail, of intoxicating drinks, in Canada, the Presbyterians are the parties who are of the three religious sections above named, *the most*, and by *far the most*, engaged in the same ?

---

* For a minute analysis and general description of wines, see Brande's Dictionary of Science, &c., 2nd edition,—at Maclear & Co., Toronto. Also see a sample of advertisements of Liquors, which can be seen among *the many*, in the newspapers in Quebec, Montreal, Ottawa, Kingston, Toronto, Hamilton and London, (the cities of Canada) herein appended.

9. When the writer came from Scotland to live "amongst the trees," in 1833, with the wigwam of the Indian near by,—and where he has heard the praises of God put forth in the Indian and in the English languages, there were then, if he recollects aright, four or five Presbyterian ministers in western Canada, north and west of and in Toronto,— the late Rev. Messrs. McGill, of Niagara, Gale, of Hamilton, Rintoul, of Toronto, and Ross, of Aldborough,—and also he thinks the late eminent Rev. Mr. Proudfoot, of London,—say five in all. Now in 1860, there are in and west and north of Toronto, Presbyterian ministers, about one hundred and seventy-two (172) in number. Has the traffic in the sales and in the drinking habits, amongst Presbyterians, decreased or increased? We have some right, surely, any one has the right, to put that question, for the *serious consideration* of the ministers of the whole Presbyterian church. There are four divisions of that church. They are at this time represented in all Canada by ministers, viz :— Church-Scotland, 111 ; Synod-Presbyterian, 145 ; United Presbyterian, 66 ; and Presbytery Stamford, 6,—in all, say 328. *

10. Again, we can suppose the following question to be put, as something similar has been put forth years ago, and perhaps not unheeded, —*is one place* (tavern, bar, saloon, or shop, as the case may be) where an unlimited sale of intoxicating drinks is licensed, working in one direction, equal to the mental and religious exertions working in another direction, *of five ministers* of religion in any locality? Again, (and in another view and the true one) if the number of places so licensed and unlicensed, in Toronto city, be divided by the number of ministers of religion, of all classes, within its bounds,—will the result *be five !!* Five grog places to each minister, *the very reverse* of one such place to five ministers,—and so likely that this proportion may be throughout the whole Province. But in reference to Toronto, (and the same in all the Province), if the places of sale are appropriated or set aside (as connected by the *sellers*) to the *three* churches named, and as there are 40 or 43 ministers and priests of these churches, officiating and not officiating, in Toronto, there will likely be *ten* such selling places *to each* of these ministers and priests 1! Again, (arithmetic and arithmetical deductions are not useless studies,) what proportion then, are *these exertions* of ministers of religion, necessarily increased or abated, joyfully exercised or with streaming tears woefully lamented, by the actions of Presbyterians, Roman Catholics and Episcopalians?

11. In Stratford, the county town of the County of Perth, (where, "when all the world's asleep," we pen these remarks,) the above calcu-

---

* The other denominations are as follows : Church-England, 810 ; Roman Catholic, 789 ;—these two with the Presbyterians, amount to 1486 ; Methodists (various) 757 ; Congregational, 72 ; Canada C. Conference, 82 ; Bible Christian 83 ; Baptists (three) 208 ; Evangelical Lutheran, 15 ; United Brethren, 9. These in all amount to 1121 ; (see Maclear & Co's Almanac, 1860.) There are also the Evangelische Association,—the Mennonist,—the Unitarians. Besides, there are the Jewish Synagogues in Montreal and Toronto.

lations are about exact :—there were 200 places in the county where intoxicating drinks were sold, and about forty ministers of religion officiating in it,—and in Stratford itself, the proportion has been as high as six and a fraction of these places to each of the seven ministers! In St. Mary's, a secularly thriving village in the county, and as prettily located as any place in Canada West,—there were about and over, eight such places for each of the six officiating ministers.* But as a whole, in this county, the proportion was and we believe is, nigh *five* as above stated! Five such places to one minister of religion! And the proportion of offences and crimes as arising from intoxicating drinks, is seventeen to eighteen cases out of every twenty cases of petty and larger offences and crimes! *And this cursed traffic, cursed by the groans and wails of women and children, was and is carried on solely and alone by Presbyterians, Episcopalians and Roman Catholics, in this County of Perth!*

12. Analyze the other forty-one counties in Upper Canada, and will the same arithmetical results be found, and with *the same* religious professors? Will there be any of the Jewish persuasion found in the traffic? Will there not also, be found in all our counties, ministers of religion—honest men of that high calling and profession,—who will declare, *that the greatest enemy and foe to their exertions*, as a whole, *is the retail liquor traffic and trade!* They have so declared to us, in our experience, Presbyterian ministers we can refer to as well,—and when we could see as we did see, the humbleness of manner, the glaze starting in the eyes, and all but the "trickle of the tear" down the cheek. These are the honest ministers of religion yet to be found in all our churches,—fighting and working hard, in their calling, with and against one great unseen devil in the human heart, and also against a proportion of five at least, open agents of an arch-Enemy seen and felt, *also* fighting and working hard in *their* calling,—and the *latter* all combined, apparently and alas! having *the mastery!*

13. But is this *increase*, increase we are lawfully to suppose,—of labours and exertions against a common foe and enemy of Christianity and of humanity, complained of by ministers of religion *other* than those of the three sectional churches referred to? We do not find that it is. How do we know? We receive, and gladly avail ourselves of our habits of early rising in perusing, almost all the religious periodicals published in Canada, *and we have never yet found a complaint*, in these papers, by Methodists, Baptists, Congregationalists, &c., against Presbyterians, Roman Catholics and Episcopalians, for creating the great and univer- sal causes, for such cruel evils as the miseries, afflictions, poverty, dis- tresses, orphanages, widowhoods, and the crimes and offences of all sorts, even murders,—for the adulteries, houses of ill-fame, Sabbath- breaking, cursing and swearing, drunkenness, tippling, indecencies,

---

* There has been hard work there in the liquor trade; an inspection of the Clerk of Peace quarterly returns of convictions will show. See also St. Mary's *Argus* of 1st and 8th December, 1859.

child disobediences, &c., &c., all of which things, (and how many more?) the liquor trade and traffic as referred to, has such a close connection with, nay *which it* engenders,—and to all which trade and traffic so carried on by Presbyterians, Roman Catholics and Episcopalians, and *the consequences* of that trade, the Methodists, Baptists, Congregationalists, &c., are exposed to! The matter resolves itself into a very simple element or axiom, namely : in the social position of the whole community, is any portion of it which is embraced as a *body* and with a *name,* responsible for its acts or the acts of its members? A single person is ;—and, a whole body, by the acts of its parts, must have *some responsibility.*

14. If the contents of this pamphlet, be put in a translated language into the hands of those we " professing christians" call the " heathen," to whom we send missionaries to,—what may l supposed to be the remarks and answers of such " heathen," upon t' habits and customs and the examples of the " christian ?" If our habits are condemned by *ourselves,* " we being the judges," in what light are we placed before the heathen, to whom we desire to introduce a pure christianly wisdom and hope,—God being our Judge ? Reader, if thou art a " professing christian," speak ?

15. Shall it be answered, that of all the anomalies, contrarieties, contradictions, and hypocrisies, which can be adduced in modern times, there will appear none so strong or so great, (the human chattel slavery and sales of the African race by professing christians in the United States and elsewhere excepted,) *there will appear none so great* as the one which " professing christians" support, in the raising up and nurturing weapons and symbols of satanic agency, *alike* destructive of heathen maxims and habits as of christian principles,—in a hateful, a sinful, and a cursed traffic in intoxicating drinks !

16. But we are to presume, that a " heathen" may and *can* say more ! *

17. The wisest and the most humane, albeit the most christianly, legislation of modern times, will appear to be that which will *prohibit* the public retail trafficing in intoxicating liquors. To inaugurate the social condition of a people for loyalty, bravery, *humanity*, and sobriety, and as conducive for the cultivation of arts and manufactures, for commercial progress and integrity, and for the advancement in education and knowledge, and above all for a *consistency* as a professedly religious people, the *crowning act* of the wise Legislature, should be,—a restrain-

---

* What has the "fire-water" (as the Indians of North America term intoxicating drink) what has it done amongst the Indian population of North and South America? It was introduced amongst them by professing christians who invaded or acquired the lands of the Indian. It has decimated or nigh annihilated them. So great indeed was the extent of the effects of the "fire-water," that the *humanity* of the Legislation of Canada was excited to pass prohibitory laws as to the Indians. If done in mercy to them, why not to be exercised in mercy *to us,* and for our wives and children ?

ing and a prohibitory law, applicable to the trade and traffic in intoxicating liquors. *

J. J. E. LINTON.

Stratford, C. W., 6th February, 1860.

PROHIBITION NOT A NEW DOCTRINE.

(From *Alliance Weekly News*, 10th December, 1859.)

In 1743, a bill was brought into Parliament for lowering the cost of licenses to retail spirituous liquors, and also the duty per gallon on those liquors. This bill passed the House of Commons, without any difficulty; but in the House of Lords it was vigorously opposed, though it was ultimately carried by a majority of 82 against 55. Some of those who voted in the minority, however, felt the matter to be of such importance, that, though they had failed in their vote, they published to the country their solemn protest against the passing of so iniquitous a measure. This protest was signed by nine bishops, and also by many noble lords.

---

* Far, far, from our intention is it, to "disparage" the unwearied exertions of so many faithful ministers of Christ in Canada, in their endeavours to stem the iniquity of the liquor traffic which surrounds them. Of course, from the tenor of our preceding remarks, we refer to ministers of the Episcopalian, Presbyterian, and Roman Catholic Churches. There are many of the ministers of the two first named churches, members of temperance organizations, and who work in the cause with "might and main." And there are those in the Roman Catholic church who have effected, amongst their people, *a great change* as to their previous habits. And we would desire to refer to the general sober habits of the *French* Canadians. We can also, as to the Roman Catholics, refer to our own locality of County of Perth, and to the untiring and humane exertions of the Rev. P. Crinnan of Stratford. We write of his exertions, from what we know and learn. Apparently, the Roman Catholic priesthood have more *power* over their people, than the Protestant have over theirs. Should not the Roman Catholic priesthood, therefore, be more anxious to help to restrain their people? Especially, if it does appear that the proportion of intemperance, as exhibited, is greater with the Roman Catholics.

There are those of the Church of England, who are among the first in the good cause of temperance, and we may refer, as an example of high worth, to Rev. J. Shortt, Port Hope, and Rev. H. Mulkins of Kingston, and to the Right Rev. the Lord Bishop of Huron (Dr. Cronyn). Of the Presbyterians, there is the champion in the cause, Rev. W. Ormiston, M.A., Hamilton, United Presbyterian, and at hand, there is that *devoted* servant of his Master, Rev. Donald McKenzie of Zorra; who has had for so many years, since 1835, the largest body of Presbyterians under the charge of any minister in Canada. And how many more, also, in the Presbyterian church. But the *evil*, as we have stated, *is still there*.

Far, then, is it from our thoughts, to cast a "disparagement." We *honour*, —we ever hope to honour while we live and breathe—the Messengers of Christ, of all denominations. We are obliged, however, to record *facts*, special and general. No good cause can be commended by "hiding the truth." Errors, when seen by those inclined to do well, with the clergy and with the people, these errors will, we trust, be remedied. They are *facts* and *acts* of man's own doing.

They protest against the bill for several reasons, amongst which was the following :—

" 4th. Because the opulence and power of a nation, depend upon the numbers, industry, and vigour of its people ; and its *liberty and happiness* on their *temperance and morality ;* to all which this bill threatens destruction, by authorizing 50.000 houses to retail a poison, which, by universal experience, is known to debilitate the strong and destroy the weak, to extinguish industry, and to inflame those intoxicated by its malignant efficacy, to perpetrate the most heinous crimes. For what confusion and calamities may not be expected, when near a twentieth part of the houses in this kingdom shall be converted into seminaries of drunkenness and profligacy, authorized and protected by the legislative power ? And as we conceive the contribution to be paid by these *infamous recesses,* and the money to ne raised by this destructive project, are considerations highly unworthy the attention of Parliament, when compared with the extensive evils from thence arising, so are we of opinion that, if the real exigencies of the public required raising the immense sum this year granted, they could by no means palliate the having recourse to a supply founded on the indulgence of debauchery, the encouragement of crime, and the destruction of the human race."

Now we think the above quotation contains the sum and substance of the whole question. The basis here laid down, is broad enough and strong enough to rest the whole temperance movement upon, both in its moral suasion and its legal prohibition aspects. Every line is full of sound scientific and moral truth though penned more than a hundred years ago.

1. The first position here taken is, *that the opulence and power of a nation depend on the numbers, industry, and vigour of its people, and that the liquor traffic is destructive of these.*

Nothing we think can be clearer than this. When a country is found decreasing in numbers, it is an infallible sign of national declension and decay. It was said by a political writer, some time since, that Turkey would by and by cease to exist, for want of Turks. Anything in a nation, therefore, that tends to destroy the lives of its people, should be regarded as a dire evil ; and this tendency the liquor traffic has. It is well known, that in England tens of thousands annually die untimely deaths through drink, and the loss this country sustains in this respect, is a loss that cannot be easily conceived. And then, again, the opulence and power of a nation depend on the *industry* of its inhabitants. Industry makes wealth, and wealth gives power. But the liquor traffic is a foe to national industry, and is therefore proportionally destructive of national wealth. Only think for a moment—sixty millions a year *spent* in drink, as the first item ; sixty millions more lost *in connection with drink,* through waste of time, destruction of property, and other causes, as the second item ; and then millions upon millions more spent in providing for paupers, taking care of lunatics, and punishing criminals, that have been made such entirely by drink ; and it must be seen how fearfully the liquor traffic tells on our national wealth and national greatness. The people of this country will always be enormously taxed and grievously impoverished, while the drinking system prevails, and England will never become great and glorious in the true sense of those words, while this iniquitous liquor traffic is allowed to exist.

2. The next position taken is, *that the liberty and happiness of a people, depend on their temperance and morality, and that strong drink destroys temperance and morality, and inflames those intoxicated by its malignant efficacy, to perpetuate the most heinous crimes.*

There can be no true liberty without temperance, and there can be no true happiness without morality. Now, the tendency of the liquor traffic is to produce intemperance, and it is therefore subversive of liberty ; its tendency is to produce immorality, and it is therefore an enemy to happiness. Intemperance makes men slaves to their appetites, and to evil passions of every kind, and it renders them unfit for and unworthy of the exercise of political power. A nation of drunkards could not govern themselves—could not provide for themselves—could not defend themselves—could neither enjoy the present life nor fit themselves for the life to come. It may truly be said, "*Far worse than brutes they live—far worse than brutes they die!*" And then intemperate men are also the means of keeping others, who are worthy of political liberty, in bondage with themselves; and as to happiness, they not only destroy their own, but they destroy the happiness of wives and children, parents and friends, and all who are connected with them as well. And with regard to crime, we need only refer to the oft-repeated testimony of our Judges on the point;—in short, the fact is well known that no crime is too heinous, and hateful, and deadly, and malignant for men to commit, when under the demonizing influence of drink. The liquor traffic, then, should have inscribed in blackened characters on its escutcheon, "*Vice, immorality and crime!—Lamentation, mourning and woe!*"

3. The next position taken is, *that public houses are seminaries of drunkenness and profligacy, and that untold confusion may be expected when a large number of such houses are authoriz d and protected by the legislative power.*

Now, every house in which intoxicating drinks are sold, is a drunkery. There may be less drunkenness in some of those houses than there is in others; but then there is drunkenness, more or less, in all. The magnificent hotel may claim to be far more respectable than the common pot-house; but if the mechanic staggers home drunk from the one, the so-called gentleman is often led home drunk from the other. There can be no doubt but that there is as much drunkenness among independent, professional and commercial men, as there is among the working classes, making due allowance for the difference in numbers. And this is by no means a matter of surprise. Strong drink will produce the same effects on the rich as on the poor; and while the common public house is open as a trap for the one class, the splendid hotel stands open as a trap for the other class. And then the public house is also a school of profligacy. Drunkenness and other bad habits generally go together. The lessons learned at the drunkery never tend towards anything good. And when large numbers of the population acquire drunken and profligate habits, sad and calamitous must be the results; and let it be borne in mind, that in proportion as drunkeries are licensed and supported by the State, in the same proportion will drunkenness and profligacy be found to prevail.

4. The next position taken is, *that the contributions paid by these infamous recesses, and the revenue raised by this destructive traffic, are considerations highly unworthy the attention of Parliament, when compared with the extensive evils thence arising.*

What is the fifteen millions of revenue now annually raised when placed in comparison with the health, happiness, and morality of the people? It ought not for one moment to be thought of. But, then, this fifteen millions need not be lost to the Government after all. What would the payment of fifteen millions revenue be to a people sober and industrious, and freed from the bondage and slavery of drink? A mere nothing! Why, they might take fifteen millions out of the sixty millions now *spent* in drink to pay it, and then there would be forty-five millions saved. And then the sixty millions now *sacrificed in connection with drink*, through loss of time, destruction of property, &c., would be saved as well; and then the millions more that are now spent on pauperism, insanity, and crime, produced by drink, would be saved in addition. We really don't know how rich the people of this country might become, and what resources the Government might be able to command, if it were not for this blighting and withering traffic in our midst. And yet, strange to say, our rulers don't perceive this; or, if they perceive it, they have not the necessary moral principle or moral courage to attempt a change.

5. The last position taken is that, *even if the revenue now raised could be raised by no other means, that would not palliate the having recourse to a supply grounded*

on the indulgence of debauchery, the encouragement of crime, and the destruction of the human race.

Better that the revenue should sink, and the Government sink with it, than the flood gates of drunkenness, and vice, and immorality should be let loose upon the land! Government, we know, is necessary; but then Government ought not to be supported by the vices of the people; on the contrary, Government should do its utmost to suppress those vices. Government has no more right to do evil that good may come than an individual has, and therefore nothing can justify the raising of any part of the national revenue as the result of national drunkenness. If the gain derived from the liquor traffic is *immoral gain*, then the part of that gain that goes into the national exchequer is as much immoral as the part that goes into the coffers of the publican, and the curse of God is as certainly upon it! We hold that it would be a disgrace, under any circumstances, for the Government to derive any part of its revenue from such a source as the liquor traffic; but doubly deep is the disgrace when it is known that the revenue could be supported better without that traffic than with it; and that, so far from being helpful to the State, its tendency in a thousand forms is to cripple, and injure, and destroy!

In conclusion, we ask—Were not the views of those bishops and noble lords just as to this matter, and have not their fearful forebodings as to coming evil been fully realized? How strange that the light then vouchsafed should have become so far obscured as that nearly a hundred years should pass away before the Temperance Reformation, the special object of which was to counteract this evil, was commenced! However, let us be thankful that the light has again dawned, that the work has commenced now, that it has proved so far successful and that it is our privilege to take part in the glorious struggle!

J. P. U.

[The above will likely be found as sound a constitutional document as has been issued on the subject, and withal in a small compass.]

SUMPTUARY LAWS.—RIGHT TO PROHIBIT.

(EXTRACTS.)

"Why should we temperance men interefere with our *sumptuary rights?*" This is a kind of ammunition commonly used by those who oppose the advocates of temperance and prohibitive and restrictive principles, forgetting, a most material forgetfulness, that *the rights* of man, as a human being, individually, when he is a "*lone*" man, in a "*lone*" place or district, are altogether different in their appliance, than when *that same* man, is in, and amidst, and forms part of, a congregated *mass* of human beings, each one of which like himself, *has rights*. Plant a man on the Sahara desert, or on the sandy plains of Mexico, or in the midst of a prairie of the west, "where the wild Buffalo roam," and his rights *there*, which he can exercise and so likely without injury to *another*, none daring to oppose, thwart, or divert them,—will be somewhat diverse from *the doing* or *exercising* of the same *rights*, on King Street, Toronto, or Great St. James Street, or McGill Street, or Papineau Square, or Place de Armes in Montreal. Why? Just imagine *what rights*, a human being can without molestation and without injury to anything around him, exercise in the desert places alluded to,—and see him exercise the same on the streets or squares above named.

"A Hindoo has or had *a right*, truly, to immolate and make burn to a crisp or to ashes, the widow of a deceased Hindoo, or to throw a smiling babe, perhaps just ushered into life,—into the river Ganges. And this simile founded on the facts and acts of other peoples, may be extended indefinitely. But let any one immolate a widow by fire on the streets or squares above named, or openly throw a babe into the Bay in Toronto, or into the flowing stream of the St. Lawrence from one of the wharves at Montreal, and what would be done, what would be thought by us, of these acts?

"Man's *rights* and restrictions are varied, increased, decreased, and assimilated, just according to the position, place, and school or class of civilization he is in,—and these rights and restrictions are regulated *by laws*,—and with us, "by laws for the public good." Each individual man and woman, now a days, in our state of civilization, in the British Empire, the highest organized state yet extant, God be praised,—must yield, he is *made* to yield, his particular inclination, be it *a right* or a "anything," must yield or relinquish such, *for the public good or weal.*

"Now as to the matter in hand, why is it that a man cannot make or manufacture, or sell, intoxicating drinks, without his *right* of doing so, being interfered with, in the shape of cash duties of excise or of license? Why is it that he cannot manufacture and sell without any hindrance? He is simply *prohibited* from doing the latter. And how many things is man prohibited and restrained from doing, because the "public good" demands and compels the prohibition and restriction.

"Is it time to prohibit and restrain the *public retail sale* of intoxicating liquors sold for *any* purpose? Is it wise in the face of the accumulated facts, obliged to be accumulated and commented on to meet opponents and demandants, is it wise even to *hesitate*, to wait, to consider such a question? It is undeniable, as a repeatedly proven fact, and I am cognisant of it as *one* witness and as a public officer of government competent to give the fact, and independent and (I trust) humane enough not to conceal it,—that of all the offences, crimes, miseries, poverties, orphanages, widowhoods, &c., which occur amongst us, a large proportion or share can be put on the said public retail sale. Of crimes, petty and larger, I unhesitatingly pronounce the proportion of those crimes to be about *seventeen to eighteen* parts out of *twenty* parts! Is that a large share? I am not a "solitary" in my investigation. The facts shewing such a large proportion, have been put forth by other responsible parties,—in Canada and in Britain. They are now beyond controversy. Has a man, have men, *the right*, to interfere with and oppose, and also to uphold sumptuary laws, in such a case:—shall the mere *idea* of a "sumptuary right," be *greater* in weight, for legislative purposes, than the above incontrovertible *fact*. It is only waste of my time, or of any sensible person's time, to repeat and go over, merely as it were, *to please* an opponent, the train of elucidatory facts referable to this matter. I may as well submit *to be obliged* to prove, that the table I am now writing at, which is a square one, is not *a round one!* The thing is too feeble, too idiotic, to be thought of. But, observe, my dear sir, that philosophically, *a man's prepossessions sometimes cause him to act idiotically!*

"As to personal ambition or selfish-ends which I may have. Whew! I have attained to the summit of my ambition here below, namely,—the power to do some good,—and again, as my income is derived, as Clerk of the Peace of this County, *from fees*, and not *salary*, (the fees are not large by any means as the C. Peace Tariff will show) and these fees besides are pretty much annihilated, in regard of a respectable and responsible office by the various changes in our laws,—and when you know (as you do) that these fees are greatly increased by petty and larger crimes,—and *these crimes* again are so increased (as above briefly referred to) by the public retail sale and traffic of intoxicating drinks,—and I am an advocate (and I hope a keen and a just one) for the doing away with *that retail* sale, thereby, as it were, "quarrelling with my bread and butter," am I selfish? Recollect that noble sentiment of a late British legislator, which he uttered in the House of Commons, and which is engraven on his tomb, the late Mr. Brotherton, M.P.,—"my wealth does not consist in the vastness of my possessions, *but in the fewness of my wants!*"

J. J. E. L.

NUMBER OF PLACES FOR RETAIL OF LIQUORS, &c., IN EACH COUNTY IN UPPER CANADA.

COST OF ADMINISTRATION OF JUSTICE, &c.

The population of the County of Perth in 1859, is believed to be 33,166 as nearly as can be ascertained by the writer (see statistics in *Examiner and Beacon*, Stratford newspapers, November, 1859); and the number of *places* in the *County* where Intoxicating drinks are sold is reckoned about 200,*—so, take the population of any one of the Counties in Upper Canada, 42 in number, and *say*,—as the population of the County of Perth being 33,000 produces 200 places of retail, what will (say county of York, or Ontario, or Peel, or Glengarry, or Lanark) population being (say the amount) produce?

What an appalling number in the aggregate of all the counties in Upper Canada will be the total result! But the proportion, when closely analysed, will be found to be greater in villages, towns and cities, than in the rural districts, in the *proportion of the population.* For instance :—in Toronto (population, say 50,000) the proportion will likely be one liquor *place* to each 125 inhabitants, young and old : in St. Mary's, (county of Perth) population 2,000, about one to each 40 inhabitants, and in Stratford, population about 3,000, about one to each 70. But for a *general* approximation, the plan above alluded to, might be safely followed for a basis, and it is believed would not be an over, but an *under* estimate.

Again,—if the *average* charge for a retail license in Upper Canada be say $28, (in towns and cities will likely be more, but such would not affect the aggregate), the aggregate value to each county may be approached. Then estimate the expences and charges in each county for a proportion of interest on cost of Gaol, Gaolers and Turnkeys salaries, Sheriff's fees, Constables, Magistrates, (petty cases) Clerk of Peace fees, County Attorney, Queen's Counsel, Jurors, Boarding Prisoners (criminal and lunatic), Firewood, &c. &c., and the *fines*,—and the *time* wasted, for which in so many instances there is no remuneration. And what shall be said as to a proportion of the Judge's salaries, Recorder's, Police Magistrates, &c. ?

---

* The population in July, 1842, when we emigrated to it, then a "wilderness," was about 200, and six stopping places there were then for travellers and emigrants, where intoxicating drinks were furnished. In 1859, in St. Mary's and Stratford alone, in this county, there were about 100 ! St. Mary's had over 60, Stratford over 40. We had the honor in 1840, in Montreal, of naming this county, which we did after the county in Scotland the first settlers came from. They settled in North Easthope. We acted as delegate for the obtaining the separation of this district of country from the county of Huron. We were also in attendance at Parliament as a delegate in 1847, for the same purpose, but did not then succeed.

Is there a profit in a money or cash value, crediting the receipts for licenses payable to the municipalities and debiting the costs, as above, attendant on the offences, crimes, &c , which latter are the results (say as 18 cases out of 20) of the liquor trade and traffic?

Is there a profit, when to the debit side are also to be carried the poverty, temporal losses, miseries, widowhoods, orphanages, offences, crimes, sabbath desecration, cursing and swearing, drunkenness and tippling, whoremongery, prostitution, &c. ?

Is there a profit? Let it appear. We have not hinted as to moral hindrances. Is there a *responsibility* applicable to those who compose majorities in councils and legislative halls, who plant with a parasitical influence *the things* which so vividly are seen *to bring on* the woes, destitutions, offences, crimes, &c., in our noble Province, which are attributable to the retail trade in intoxicating drinks.

20th January, 1860.

CONVICTIONS FOR OFFENCES, &c., COUNTY OF PERTH.

We have it in our power to state the number of convictions for offences, &c , being the petty cases before magistrates from the time (January, 1853), when this county was finally set apart from the county of Huron, but we content ourselves with an abstract of, say the last two years. The returns are published quarterly by the Clerk of the Peace.

For quarter, or 90 days ending,	March, 1858	....	102
" "	June, "	....	173
" "	Sept. "	....	183
" "	Dec. "	....	138
" "	March, 1859.	....	95
" "	June "	....	150
" "	Sept. "	....	87
" "	Dec. "	....	139
			1067

We have no hesitation in stating, as a public officer, that if the inducements and temptations of the common public *retail* of spirituous and other intoxicating drinks were removed, there would *not* be the same number of offences, &c.

There are, no doubt, cases for recovery of wages included in the above abstract, but as a whole, my experience leads me to state *positively* as to the *causes* of offences, &c , being in the unnecessary public temptations to drink, and the proportion of *such* cases is about 17 to 18 out of every 20 cases.

Again, in the above convictions are *not* included the cases tried before the Quarter Sessions or the Assizes; and the observation and experience of observing persons will show how many of such cases are directly traceable to " drink." Some of the severest cases for assault and injury, tried at the Quarter Sessions, were owing to " drink." Nay, the variety of cases so traceable, embrace civil suits as well. Where, then, we may lawfully enquire, has not this evil traffic an influence?

We submit to any one who ponders on the *condition* of society, any where, that it will appear as a very common-place thought for us to state, that if such temptations as are in this retail trade, (of man's own creating), were removed, there would be every scope for religious and moral training. In fact, to the serious thinker and observer, will occur, this sad thought,—and to be recorded in the latter part of the nineteenth century, that " christianity has not had fair play." Are we to infer, always to think on the devil's side, that " let us wait, God will interfere." True His power is present, but he has instructed us to use *means*, and as our Saviour anointed the blind man's eyes before restoring them to see,—so that was a token to us to use *means*; but the retail trade and traffic in inflaming and exciting drinks, is *not* a means for His Glory, or for the good of mankind.

Our *duty* as a " professing christian people" is too apparent even for the most ignorant and untaught *not* to comprehend. Do the poverty, misery, afflictions, offences, &c., &c., traceable to intoxicating drinks, conduce to the glory of God? Do they conduce or lead *to our shame* as a people? The following remarks as to " *our duty*," in a respectable newspaper, which is an advocate of *humanity*, have come before us while compiling the above abstract of convictions, and we give the same a currency in these pages. May they be seriously thought upon :

" Did you ever notice that the Holy Evangelists agree in representing " Our Saviour as more severe in His denunciations against the Phari- " sees, than against either the Sadducees, who were sceptical, or the " Publicans who were immoral? Did you ever notice what sort of " offences, among the Pharisees, gave reasons to this severity of denun- " ciation? It was their presentation, before God and man, of a *pro- " fession* and certain outward manifestations of *piety*, as a substitute " for the performance of *duty*. They were pre-eminently the pious " people of their age and nation. The sabbaths, prayers, fasts, bap- " tisms and other ritual observances, by a punctilious devotion to which " they distinguished themselves, were all commanded in their law, yet " these, as well as the oppression and extortion which they practised, " appear conspicuously as counts in the indictment brought by our " Saviour against them. The same vice exists, and just as conspicuous- " ly. among the same class of people amongst us now. The display of " piety, by itself alone, *as a substitute for the performance of duty*, is " not only practised but inculcated, apparently to an observer, for the " purpose of opposing or passing by, the most urgently needed reforms."

25th January, 1860.

CRIME IN TORONTO.

ABSTRACT FROM THE STATISTICAL REPORT OF CRIME IN THE CITY OF TORONTO, DURING THE YEAR 1859.

Number of offenders apprehended and brought before the Police Magistrate upon the following charges:—Cutting and wounding, 6 males; highway robbery, 14 males; housebreaking, 15 males; arson, 9 males, 2 females; passing counterfeit money, 13 males, 4 females; obtaining goods under false pretences, 8 males, 9 females; cattle stealing, 8 males; gambling, 8 males; rape, 4; receiving stolen goods, 18 males, 21 females; forgery, 11 males, 4 females; compounding felony, 1 male; larceny, or suspicion of larceny, 484 males, 207 females, 40 boys; assault, 398 males, 55 females; assaulting police, 23 males : drunk and disorderly, 1,201 males, 954 females, 117 boys; indecent exposure, 4 males; keeping disorderly house or found in them, 80 males, 74 females; child desertion, 6 females, ; selling spirits without license, &c., 72 males, 9 females; breach of city law, 351 males, 29 females; threatening, 77 males, 50 females; carrying or selling unlawful weapons, 7 males, 1 female; trespass, 76 males, 28 females; keeping dangerous dogs, 21 males; cruelty to animals, 12 males; contempt of court, 10 males; furious driving, 8 males; deserting employment, 15 males; non-payment of wages, 35 males. Total, 2,918 males, 1,518 females, 157 boys, (40 arrested for larceny or on suspicion, and 117 for drunkenness, or other disorderly conduct,—in all, 157 boys.) Grand total, 4,593.

HOW DISPOSED OF.

These were disposed of in the following manner:—Committed to goal for one month or under, 375 males, 718 females. Committed to gaol for six months or under, 64 males, 45 females. Fined or imprisoned, 723 males, 88 females. Summarily punished by fines, 383 males, 15 females; committed for trial, 66 males, 15 females. Bound over to keep the peace, 63 males, 30 females. Committed in default of sureties, 28 males, 17 females. Remanded, 561 males, 228 females. Dismissed, 123 males, 27 females. Charges withdrawn, 206 males, 27 females. Prisoners discharged, 558 males, 286 females.

NATIVE COUNTRIES OF PRISONERS.

Of the prisoners 1,767 males, and 1,175 females were Irish; 455 males, 155 females were Canadian; 378 males, and 73 females were English; 142 males, and 25 females were Scotch; 65 males, and 13 females were Americans; 43 males, and 7 females were Germans; 103 males, and 14 females were coloured; 177 males, and 31 females were from other countries.

AGES OF PRISONERS.

From ten to fifteen years, 117 males and 7 females; from fifteen to twenty years, 225 males and 98 females; from twenty to thirty, 896 males and 637 females; from thirty to forty, 803 males and 374 females; from forty to fifty, 720 males and 219 females; from fifty to sixty, 196 males and 159 females; from sixty to seventy, 54 males and 23 females; from seventy to eighty, 4 males and 1 female.

NUMBER OF CONVICTIONS.

Of the male prisoners 59 have been confined twice; 72 three times; 23 four times : 11 five times; 18 six times; 2 seven times; 1 ten times, and 1 eleven times during the year.

Of the female prisoners, 85 have been confined twice; 39 three times; 24 four times; 30 five times; 18 six times; 24 seven times; 15 eight times; 5 nine times; 1 ten times; and 1 eleven times during the year."

The above abstract of crime in Toronto city appeared in the two city newspapers, the *Globe* and the *Leader*, 16th and 17th January, 1860, and any reader of these two well edited papers, cannot fail, in the course of investigation for a period, *to see* in the records given, the close connection between offences, crimes, follies, destitutions, &c , and the retail trade in liquors. The evidence is beyond cavil; and if other newspapers are consulted in the various counties, the results of investigation will be the same. The "anxiety" of temperance and prohibition advocates, in producing proof, is not met with an equal frankness by their opponents, who are ever *over-careful* for a reform, and very economical in their "admissions!"

How many of the cases of the above abstracted 4,593 cases for 1859 will be found closely, indirectly, and remotely, allied to the traffic in liquors?

Again, in a separate table in the *Leader* of the 13th January, appears *commitments* for 1859 to Toronto Gaol, furnished by the gaoler, Mr. Allen, we presume. The table is a long one—more so than the above—and appears to be prepared with much care. We extract only the following :

The number of prisoners committed was 2,085, namely, 1,120 males, and 965 females. The religious denominations to which they belong are : Roman Catholics, 1,008 ; Church of England, 734 ; Presbyterians, 141 ; Methodists, 92 ; Baptists, 15 ; other denominations, 9 ; no denomination, 26. There were committed of the above, *once*, 1805 : the others were committed *twice*, and so on. There were 90 under 15 years of age ; from 15 to 20, 386 ; 20 to 30, 839 ; 30 to 40, 468 ; above 40, 352. The *national* and the *trade* divisions are also given, and the degree of education : there being of the latter 684 could neither read nor write ; 572 could read only ; 783 could read and write imperfectly ; 40 males could read and write well, and 0 of a superior education. As "drunk and disorderly," there are 724 males, and 805 females (1529). It is added, "Of the female prisoners there were married, 152 ; widows, 80 ; servants, 110 ; and prostitutes, 671 !" The population of Toronto is about 50,000.

We ask, what influence or connection had the liquor trade or traffic in Toronto with all these cases?

CRIME IN MONTREAL.

(From the Family Herald, 25th January,—a useful Weekly Paper.)

" The Annual Report of the Chief of Police presents rather an alarming state of affairs. During the year no fewer than 6,881 pe sons have been arrested by the police, and brought up for trial—an increase of 1,407 over the arrests of last year. Of this number 5,113 were males, and 1,768 females ; while of the whole number 3,221 were arrested for drunkenness in its various stages, of ' tippling. drunk, drunk and disorderly.' To this number would require to be added 558 classed under the head, " breach of the peace," for it is well known to any one who has studied life, in this its lowest phase, that nine out of every ten breaches of the peace are caused by drink. There are 210 classed as " impeding and incommoding," which we profess not to be able to define, but that 210 might with safety be placed to the previous. number, which makes the total number of drunk and disorderly in their various stages, from the incipient, which is styled by the Chief of Police as tippling—a stage of drinking we had always considered beyond the precincts of magisterial jurisdiction—up to the confirmed stage, classed as impeding and incommoding, 3,989. In fact, the bulk of the crime may be set down as resulting from drunkenness. The graver offences against the law were, murder 1, highway robbery 2, receiving stolen goods 5, larceny 226, gambling 3, and various other recognizable offences include a certain portion of the number; but that is small when compared with the list of drunkenness—a state of things no one would believe when they listen to the flimsy harangues of some of our loquacious demagogues. The various nationalities are represented as Irish, 3,367; French Canadians, 1,726; English, 323; Scotch, 537; British Canadian, 212; United States, 101; other countries, 109. The table seems very carefully compiled, and reflects credit upon the Chief of Police."

There is a very exact condensation of this Police Report in the *Life Boat*, of 3rd February, published at Montreal by Mr. Rose, received too late to avail ourselves of its abstract of offences. We can only refer to it.

The Montreal *Witness* commenting on the above report of the Chief of Police, Capt. M. J. Huys, states :—

" The Official Statistics in Lower Canada never state the creed of criminals, as is done in Western Canada and the United States. * * * * The whole number classed as Irish, and as French Canadians, may be considered as Roman Catholics, for if there be a few Protestants among the Irish, there will probably be an equal number of Roman Catholics in the other nationalities. We have, then, the enormous disproportion of 5,093 Roman Catholics arrested to 1,778 Protestants, or about 8 to 1. * * * What a comment this on the liquor traffic !" (The preponderance of the Roman Catholic population may account so far for this disproportion.) The population of Montreal, it is said, is about 75,000.

CRIME IN QUEBEC, C. E. AND HAMILTON, C. W.

The statistics of crime in Quebec give the whole number of persons arrested for various offences during the year 1859, at 2,294. In the City of Hamilton, C. W., the cases of various offences before the Police Magistrate for 1859, were 1,816, and of these there were 408 females.

But of crimes, higher offences, &c., before the Assize Courts and Courts of Quarter Sessions, and Recorders' Courts, the above returns do not embrace them. Their number in Counties and Cities, independent of the cases of Police Courts, are not, it is to be lamented, inconsiderable; and when arising from the traffic in intoxicating drink, should induce a *thought* for some remedy. The population of Quebec supposed to be 60,000, and Hamilton 30,000.

THE SUPPORT OF THE POOR OF CITIES—STRIKE AT ITS CAUSE— THE LICENSE SYSTEM—THE THREE GREAT EVILS OF MODERN SOCIETY.

(*To the Editor of the Globe.*)

Sir,—In your issue of the 29th December, I observed a communication as well as an able article, on the all-absorbing question of the support of the poor. Several letters have since appeared in your columns on the same subject. The question of how the poor of American cities are to be best provided for, is one agitating all parts of British America and the American States. The Americans, like ourselves, have a debased and miserable poor to support. Common humanity and religion require every community to see that the poor shall not go uncared for. Year after year the subject, at this season, comes up prominently before the public, and so it will continue to be, if some wise remedy be not found for the evil. I do not see *the true cause* of this state of things in our cities pointed out, either in your article or the communications alluded to. Had it been so, I would not have troubled you with this letter. Now, sir, what is the cause of the great portion, I may say safely three-fourths, of the poverty in our midst? The answer is on the tongue of every thinking person. The LOW GROG SHOPS, GROCERIES, and SALOONS that meet the eye in dozens, on all of our corners, up and down our best and worst streets. Every vicinity, the most secluded streets in the far-off suburbs, and the best streets and busiest thoroughfares, equally swarm with tippling bar-rooms, or little groceries, where they sell a quarter of a pound of tea or sugar, and a GALLON of WHISKEY or BEER. These back street groceries or saloons, are the resort of the poor man or his wife. Did I say his wife? Alas! that it is so: for there are too many instances in our midst of drunken wives. Hither the labouring men go after their day's work, or thither they send their little children, to purchase by the quart what breeds quarrels in their families, causes diseases and weakness, and ultimately poverty and death. The debauch of the previous night unfits the man for work and disarranges his family affairs, demoralizes his children, and, too often, causes the laboring man to lose his place. He becomes idle or sick, his wife follows his example, and the poor family, once comparatively happy, is turned into a scene of misery and squalid poverty. The children go round the streets to beg—the daughters figure in the Brook's Bush gang—Stanley-street rows, or fill up the beastly scenes, alas, poor women! of our Police Court. Can there be anything to the human heart more pitiable than to see the many fallen and drunken females who, from week to week, infest our Police Court! The poor man drinks. He spends his pennies, that should go for bread or meat, in the low saloon: he injures his health: his wife and children ultimately follow his example, or, having no one to provide for them, become beggars. Let us but examine more than half the beggars who come to our doors, and we see immediately the cause of their degradation. Let us watch the Police Courts, and examine into the cause of the quarrels and disputes that arise in our city—what is it? I need not here Sir, allude to the quarterly presentments of grand juries—to the addresses of Judges from the bench, to the calendars of our gaol—for they all teem with proofs that the *license system* is the great curse of the age in which we live.

Then the cause of the poverty in our city in a great measure is traceable to the *unchristian and inhuman* system of allowing so many liquor-selling groceries and saloons to infest our city. The benevolent societies in our midst, our Magdalen Home, Orphans' Home, Poor House, Gaol Board, the funds of all our national societies, are more or less drained and squandered in counteracting the effects on society of the deadly poison of liquor-selling and tippling !

The generous and humane are called upon thus against their will indirectly to sustain the beastly resorts of the low liquor-venders. Now, if the community *is only manly and bold enough* to face this evil, we can soon abate much of our poverty and beggary.

I see that you say in your issue of the 30th December, that the number of Inns or saloons licensed in 1859 is much smaller than that of 1858. Let the year 1860 see a much greater reduction. Where there are now three licenses given, let but one be issued ; and so year after year reduce the number until we have a sober and quiet community. Let us have the houses of the poor, if they be humble, the abodes of quietness, sobriety, and Christian feeling. It is no disgrace to be poor. The eye of God is over on the struggling and deserving poor, and *He* will secretly provide for their wants. But, if to poverty the poor man or woman adds drunkenness, profanity and crime—oh, how fallen ! Yet even for them society must care. Our city of Toronto is but a larger example of other Canadian towns and cities—Montreal and Quebec are counterparts of our community. The citizens of Toronto were lately in the midst of their civic elections, but I fear omitted to vote for the men who would try to abate the license system. Those returned as civic members are generally favourable to the system ; we must, then, rely upon private effort. We profess to be a Christian community, our city is full of elegant churches, with large and attentive audiences, where the blessed precepts of the Redeemer of the world are ably preached—we profess to believe as a people that the human soul is of immortal value, destined to live for ever ; yet I fear we read day after day with too little feeling of the most heart-rending deaths, sudden and unprepared for in our midst, the effects of drunkenness. A Coroner calls a jury on the death of some poor female or man found dead, the victim of intemperance ; it is passed over, and no more is thought of it, until some other sad tale again awakens a sympathising sigh. *Do Christian ministers feel their responsibility on the subject of the drinking usages of society ?* Are they awake to this evil in our city and in all cities ? I fear not, or more active measures would be taken to put it down.— According to their doctrines, every soul that dies is of inestimable value ; and we are very plainly told that the drunkard cannot inherit eternal life. The watchmen of Zion's glory should battle everywhere against this evil as the great power of Satan on earth. They profess to believe in the spirit power of Satan to do evil ; let ministers of religion behold the thousands of tombs that fill our land, in which rest the dust of the poor inebriate !

The three great evils of modern society are the licensing of taverns, in which poisonous liquors are sold ; the debasement of women in our great cities, which is to a certain extent caused by the first,—and the gaming-table. The three are inseparable companions, and are deadly foes to Christian progress—to hopes of happiness beyond the grave. They are the deadliest foes to human prosperity, ever looking at human society with the eye of a Sadiluceo. If we strike down the first, *the great upas tree of intemperance*, the roots that lie under it and are nourished by it will in due time die too, or at least will vanish beneath the effulgence of Christian truth and benevolence.

C. M. D.

Toronto, Jan. 21, 1860.

The above letter appeared in the Toronto *Globe* of the 27th January, and we would try to draw some attention to the statements in it. We hope there is not a thinking man or woman in Canada, but will echo the desires and the facts of this humane writer. And if we look to the social state of our Towns and Incorporated Villages, we will find the statements, in their degree, applicable to them as well as to the Cities. Such statements cannot be gainsayed.

We need not dilate. We had intended to have at some length referred to the very subject embraced in the above letter. We have observed it while preparing these sheets, and we gladly avail ourselves of its just views. We have only from all our observations and facts, to endorse the humane writer's appeals.

We had observed a good article in the *Globe* on the subject of Benevolence and the Poor; and also, that the Rev. Dr. Willis, Rev. Mr. Hope, also Rev. Dr. Fyfe, all of Toronto, have alluded to the subject impressively enough, but excepting the latter reverend gentleman, there has been no sufficient allusion to what we would call *the marrow* of the matter, till the above letter of C. M. D. appeared. Dr. Fyfe very justly remarks as follows, as regards the effects of the liquor traffic in *creating the poor*:—" I have another objection to a legal provision, in " which, perhaps, a greater number of benevolent people in this city " sympathise with me. I object to making legal provision for the poor " in Toronto, whilst legal permission for the manufacture of four-fifths " of all the poor in Toronto is continued. The city derives a revenue " from the process by which the majority of the poor are brought into " existence. And it seems nothing more than fair for us in the city to " say, if you wish to tax us to support the poor, then cease manufac- " turing them with your saloons and grog shops, or else apply the pro- " ceeds of your tavern licenses to help the families of those who spend " their all in such places. I say nothing now of the heavy tax imposed " upon the citizens of Toronto to support Police Courts, Law, &c., di- " rectly required as the result of the drinking protected and fostered " by the municipal law; but I merely object to have *a tax* to support " the poor, also chiefly made by the same means." We might differ with Dr. Fyfe as to *a legal* provision for the poor. The Municipal Act of 22 Vic. cap. 99. (1858) has provided for the wants of the necessitous poor, *if it would be acted upon.* The poor ought to be provided for, be the way what it may, but let all generous and humane hearts work and labour *to reduce the causes which create poverty.*

We might refer to as good and as high an authority as is in Canada, the Hon. G. W. Allan, M. L. C., of Toronto, and *his experience*, we are certain, will show that there are causes in our midst, *of man's own creating*, which rear up a large proportion of the poor and destitute cases which seek relief. We have before us the Report of the Protestant Magdalen Asylum of Montreal, (see *Witness* of 25th January) and in it there is evidence of what *that* causes, which thoughtless man creates. Let us examine all the Reports of our Benevolent Institutions and Societies, and *in the cases* which form the pious and humane care of their managers and visitors, we shall see *the fruits* of what " man creates." The evidence to be brought forward from all these sources, besides what is produced in the Police and Recorders Courts, Quarter Sessions and Assizes, all such is overwhelming. *We are blind.*

We can only refer to a very important letter in the Toronto *Globe* of February 2nd, by a correspondent signing " Scrutator," who is a physician, corroborative of the above letter of C. M. D.; and in the same paper there is a letter signed " A Friend to Society, " on the " Statistics of Intemperance and its results." These letters we intended to have inserted, as they are important in showing further proof. They are worthy of being consulted.

LIQUOR MANUFACTURE IN TORONTO, C. W.

The city has already become famous for the excellence of its ale. The manufacture is rapidly growing into one of importance. There are at present eight breweries in active operation in the city and vicinity, the consumption of malt in which, is over 80,000 bushels per annum The manufacture of beer does not fall short of 720,000 gallons, valued at $160,000. The principal brewers are Messrs. George and Henry Severn, of Yorkville; John A. Aldwell, Victoria Brewery; Thos. Davis, Yonge-street; Wallace and Moss, W. Copeland, Jun., Rowell & Payne, C. Thompson, and Thos. Davis, Jun.

A very extensive brewery has been erected during the year by Mr. Aldwell, on William-street, near the College Avenue, which will be one of the most complete establishments of the kind in the Province. He has spared no money in introducing all the latest improvments, and his enterprise entitles him to success.

The manufacture of whiskey has also grown to be one of considerable importance. While, unhappily, the consumption has increased in the country, the importations have very much diminished, as will be seen by the following—being the Custom House returns of the quantity of whiskey entered for consumption at this Port for the past four years.

	Gallons.	Value.
1856	75.786	$31,416
1857	12,220	4,472
1858	6,917	2,671
1859	531	360

The country from the Ottawa to the Detroit rivers, is now principally supplied by Toronto distilleries, and during the coming year the production will be largely augmented by the completion of the distillery of Messrs. Gooderham and Worts. The home market is already supplied, and it is the intention of this enterprising firm to export to England the great bulk of their increased manufacture. They will, of course, make a much superior description of whiskey than that sold here, and no doubt will create a profitable trade. When complete, they can turn out 150 barrels of 40 O. P. whiskey per day. It is expected they will require half a million of bushels annually of Western grain, besides what they can get in our own markets.

The above we extract from the *Annual Review* of the trade of Toronto in the *Globe* of the 25th January, 1860. We re-publish it for the purpose of bringing it prominently by itself before the people of Canada. If *the trade* of the manufacture of liquors in Montreal, at Kingston, Preston, St. Catherines, Chippewa, Amherstburg and some other places was also brought forward, the extent of the *inducements* for the *retail* trade, would be seen in its *largeness.* We say nothing of the importation or exportation or the wholesale trade. We say nothing here as to the manufacture and the trade being carried on by Presbyterians, Episcopalians and Roman Catholics !

We ask this question,—What good morally, religiously and socially, to Toronto, does the above "Liquor Manufacture," in its city, accomplish ?

ADULTERATED LIQUORS.

"Dr. Hiram Cox, the Cincinnati Inspector, has published many deeply interesting facts of his experience in testing liquors sold in that city. In 600 inspections of Stores and lots of liquor in every variety, he found that 90 per cent were impregnated with the most pernicious and poisonous ingredients. Nineteen young men, all sons of respectable citizens, were killed outright by only three months drinking of these poisoned liquors. Many older men, who were only moderate drinkers, died within the same period of *delirium tremens*, brought on in one quarter the time usual, even with confirmed drunkards, by drinking this same poison. Of 400 insane patients, he found that two-thirds had lost their reason from that cause,—many of them were boys under age. One boy of 17 was made insane by the poison from being drunk only once. Seeing two men drinking in a grog-shop, and that the whiskey was so strong that it actually caused tears to flow from the eyes of one of them, the Dr. obtained some of it and applied his tests. He found it to contain only 17 per cent. of alcohol, when it should have contained 40, and that the difference was supplied by sulphuric acid, red pepper, caustic, potasso and strychnine. A pint of this liquor contained enough poison to kill the strongest man. The man who had manufactured it had grown wealthy by producing it."—(*Scientific American*, and copied into the *Pilot*, and several Canadian papers.)

We would also recommend to any who may entertain a doubt, as to adulterations, the valuable paper by E. C. Delavan, Esq., of Albany, N. Y., June, 1857, extracts from the same, with a valuable appendix, including an excellent address by Bishop Potter, where also the adulterations are noted, will be found in "Lectures on Temperance," by Dr. Nott, edited by Amasa McCoy, Esq., of Albany, N. Y., (Hamilton, C.W. edition by Moffat & Co., 1858), pp. 371. This book ought to be consulted by any one desirous of advancing the progress of society in this cause.

There is an article on "Adulterations of Liquors," copied into the Montreal *Witness* of 19th October, 1859, from " Boston Journal, " *which we advise all drinkers* of Port Wine, Brandies, Gin, " Bourbon Whiskey" or other Whiskies, Rum, Wines, &c. &c., *to read..* There is enough of proof referred to there as ought to satisfy any person. *

---

* We call on our readers to peruse the "astounding disclosures" in a letter by Dr. Cox of Cincinnati, just published in Montreal *Witness* of 4th February. It will be found at the end of these pages.

REVELATIONS OF THE RETAIL TRAFFIC BY THE NEWSPAPER PRESS.

To a reader of many of our Canadian newspapers, wherein are recorded *local* events as well as those occurring at a *distance*, it requires no great aptitude in an enquirer to see in these useful papers the great influence which the retail trade in intoxicating drinks bears on the social state of man and woman. It is, we are inclined to think, very harassing to the feelings of the humane, the philanthropic, and the professing Christian, to see the records of so many cases of miseries, offences, crimes, &s., caused by *the contact* of that trade with mankind. It must be more so when there is no *practically available* recourse for a sweeping alleviation. There appears to be none, except in the doing away with the means of contact, namely : the exposure for public sale by retail, of an article which has been proved over and over again, by its seductive hold and attraction on certain parts of the constituted human frame-work, *as one dangerous to society.* But resist that contact? Some may unthinkingly, nay ignorantly, say so, —but as the *" iron will "* in man or woman, when exposed to such a contact, held up so vividly to us by habits and by *legal* sanction as *apparently* innocent, when that " iron will" is not of our own creating, but when the cause of contact and the temptation, *are ours,*—it is only folly to say "resist." The *history* of the *contact* with the " article " so dangerous, is an ample, alas ! too sad, refutation of all "advisory measures." Why have we, as a people, that article so exposed, as to tempt the trial of its efficacy for good or evil, obtainable as it is in its cost for a few coppers or pence, or for any sum ? Why put, by exposure for sale, such a disastrous temptation in the path of men and women, and of our children ?

No stronger evidence, and withal respectable and so reliable, to be adduced before our legislators for a repeal of the right to sell by retail such a dangerous commodity as intoxicating drink, does exist, next to the records themselves and *the sight* of the evils, than in the fyles of the *Newspaper Press of Canada.*

OPINIONS OF MEDICAL GENTLEMEN, CLERGYMEN, &c.

It is no object of ours unnecessarily to bring forward proofs. A very little trouble, now-a-days, with an ordinary energy, to "call" from the periodical press, would furnish a set of volumes to illustrate the iniquity of the traffic, as causing every species of crime, offence, murder, misery, poverty, &c.

We quote the opinion of the Medical Gentlemen of the Faculty of New York State, which was unanimously given, of date 4th February, 18 7 :—" Resolved, That in view of the ravages made upon the " morals, health and property of the people of this State by the use of " alcoholic drinks, it is the opinion of this Medical Society that the

" moral, sanitary and pecuniary condition of the State would be pro-
" moted by the passage of a Prohibitory Liquor Law." It will be
recollected that the opinion of the Medical gentlemen of Great Britain
was given and published years ago, against the use of intoxicating
drinks as a beverage, &c. The Medical testimony of various kinds
against such drinks is indisputable.

Very lately, this last Fall, the valuable testimony of the Clergymen
in England of the Church of England was published in Canada and
the United States, being "An address to the Clergy of the Church of
England, from members of their own body," and was signed by 112
Clergymen, the Very Rev. Francis Close, D.D., Dean of Carlisle, being
the first signer. Many other names have since been signed to this Address in England and Wales. The following are extracts :—" Whilst
" heartily thankful to the Almighty God for the efforts which are being
" made in our day for the religious and social improvement of the people
" in this land, we cannot close our eyes to the fact, that at the same time
" an *agency* is at work which well nigh nullifies them all, we refer to the
" drinking usages of society ; against which, and everything that tends
" to foster this fertile source of evil, we desire to send forth our earnest
" and conscientious protest. Parliamentary Reports, Registrars' Re-
" turns, the evidence of the Commissioners of Lunacy, of Parish
" Relieving Officers, of Physicians in Hospitals, of Chaplains in Gaols,
" as likewise the strong language of our Judges on the Bench, all
" unite in testifying that the *prolific generator* of the varied crime and
" misery by which we are surrounded *is intoxicating drink*. On this
" point no difference of opinion exists. The fact is patent and every-
" where confessed. What then are we, the Ministers of the National
" Church, doing to counteract this frightful and wide-spread evil ?"
"* * * We abstain ourselves because we believe that the drunken-
" ness which prevails may be traced back to *moderate drinking* and its
" great cause. We are convinced that moderate drinking, and not drunk-
" enness only, *supports the traffic*, the traffic tends to foster drunkenness,
" and drunkenness produces bodily misery, social degradation and spirit-
" ual death. So long as drink is supplied there will be drunkenness.
" Which is most in accordance with common sense, to supply *the cause*
" and labour in vain to remove *the effect ;* or to get rid of the effect
" through the banishment of the cause ?" * * * " We appeal to
" you, brethren, is it not drink, above all things, which tends to nullify
" the preaching of the Word, which keeps back numbers from the house
" of God, which degrades the masses of society, and mars almost every
" effort to win souls to Christ ?" Witness also the additional testimony
by the Dean of Carlisle, Dr. Close :—" If I had a thousand hands
" they should be lifted up against the cruel destroyer, drink ! I am
" persuaded, after long experience and much thought, that nothing less
" than total abstinence and a *restrictive law* will stem the fearful tor-
" rent of intoxication. Moderation is the first step towards excess,
" and its foster-father. The drunkard does less towards promoting
" drunkenness than the temperate man. The former makes drink dis-
" gusting, *the latter recommends it*." But to crown the whole, going

3

back two years, to June 1857, at Manchester, England, we find a Conference of Ministers of all denominations, Church of England, Wesleyan, Presbyterian, Independent, Baptist, &c., to the number of 1724, signing a declaration " to encourage every legitimate effort for the entire " suppression of the trade, by the power of the national will, and " through the form of a legislative enactment."—Journal of A. T.Union, N.Y., October, 1859.

Also a Convention of the Ministers at Halifax, N. S., 25th October, 1859, resolved as follows: "That as this Province is still being deeply " injured in all its real interests by the present legally authorised sale " and the very general use of intoxicating drinks, it is highly expedient " that application be made to the Provincial Parliament in its ensuing " Session, for the enactment of a law directly prohibiting their sale."

The Synod of the Reformed Presbyterian Church in Ireland in 1859, and also the Synod of the United Presbyterian Church in Scotland in 1859, resolved against the traffic. The Synod of the Presbyterian Church in Canada has also declared against intoxicating drinks. The U. Presbyterian Synod in Canada, in June, 1858, did the same. The Presbyterians in Canada are *largely* engaged in this crime and misery producing traffic, as elsewhere more fully stated by us.

At the Annual Meeting in Great Britain in 1859 of the Association for the Promotion of Social Science, declarations were made against the evils, crimes, &c., resulting from the traffic, and the memorable declarations at that meeting of the ablest man in England, Lord Brougham, have been copied into our Canadian papers, and we need not here reproduce them. They were worthy of such a noble and able man. To any one who has access to the " *Alliance Weekly News,*" published at John Dalton Street, Manchester, (Eng.,) the organ of the influential Temperance Body in England,—" *The United Kingdom Alliance,*" (Sir Walter C. Trevelyan, Bart., President,) the proceedings at the above Association will be there seen at some length. The Alliance *News* stands foremost in Britain in its advocacy for a permissive and prohibitory law. The talent shown in that paper is of no ordinary kind.

We have only to refer to the pages of the " *Canada Temperance Advocate,*" published by Mr. Becket at Montreal, (now in the 26th yearly volume,) also to the " *Life Boat,*" published by Mr. H. Rose, Montreal, (now in its 6th volume,) and to the " *Journal of the American Temperance Union,*" New York, now in its 24th volume, (Rev. Dr. Marsh, Editor,) for statistics and other similar matter, for a confirmation of what we have feebly urged in these pages, as to the *necessity* for a Prohibitory Liquor Law of *some kind*. In Great Britain there are various authentic periodicals to refer to,—The *News*, as above, " *The Temperance Star,*" published in London; also " *The Temperance Spectator,*" published there, (vol. 1 contains a library of information); the " *British Workman;*" the " *Band of Hope Review,*" published there also; the " *Western Temperance Herald,*" published at Bristol; " *The North of England League Temperance Register;*" " *The*

Guernsey League Banner," Channel Islands; "*The Temperance Monthly Visitor,*" published by Jarold & Sons, Norwich, (a paper doing good;) the "*Weekly Journal*" of the Scottish Temperance League, Hope-street, Glasgow; and there are many other avenues of the press in Britain, and by reliable public lecturers, for conveying *facts* and arguments to the public,—and *there*, in Britain, *they are much needed*,—for there is in Britain a large, influential and wealthy class engaged in the traffic of intoxicating drinks, who are opponents to the social and religious reform of this iniquitous and cruel curse. Such is to be regretted. It will be admitted by all those conversant with the matter, that in Canada we are far, far in advance of the mother country as to progress and prospects in this cause; and heartily glad are we to record it. We have *already* a "Permissive Law" in our Municipal Act of Upper Canada, and it is only for such a "Permission" that the friends of the cause are labouring in England. The monied interest in the traffic there, the vested rights of parties, the "heathen blindness," as it were, amongst an otherwise enlightened people, to keep up the *causes* of misery, poverty, crime, &c., amongst the people, are such, as by their use, should make a Briton and a Christian blush !

We add, as in papers just received, (*Alliance News* of 28th January and February 11,) that upwards of 350 ministers of the Church of England, in Ireland, have adhered to the "Ministerial Declaration;" and an address, published by 212 Baptist ministers, (22 of them resident in Scotland,) and adhered to by upwards of 100 Baptist students, in favor of entire abstinence and prohibition.

[We cut the following extract from the *Morning Chronicle* of Quebec, of the 18th February, 1859, and we do so *to show* the results of the liquor retail traffic. God forbid that our noble Province will ever show in the dense population of any of our cities, any approach to the description below. Yet let us *beware*, for unless a restraint and prohibition, is made in Canada, and that *now in time*,—we have no guarantee for what results shall follow. Years by gone, with every means of increase of moral and religious agency in New York, who would have foretold of what is described in this extract ?]

A DISSECTED PLAGUE SPOT.
(From the *New York Courier and Enquirer*.)

Notwithstanding the grievously imperfect and unfaithful administration of justice amongst us, word comes that Sing Sing is absolutely over crowded with the number of city convicts; and the same is in a great measure true of all our city and country penal establishments. Our criminal Courts are burdened with business. Our citizens have stood aghast at the rapid rate at which Pauperism, Rowdyism, and Crime, have increased from year to year; until the despairing thought has seized many minds that general demoralisation is inevitable. But how few have studied the causes of our disorganised condition ? In medicine, correct diagnosis is half a cure. In morals, we need to know what and where the evil is; the remedy will follow.

A suggestive pamphlet has been laid on our table, which exposes the extent, accessories, and economical and moral bearings of the Sunday Liquor Traffic; and we see not how any one can rise from its perusal without the conviction that a large part of our civic and social evils have here been traced to their source.

Nor will this conviction be weakened by the tone of moderation and dignity, characterizing this document of the Sabbath Committee. When such men as compose that Committee speak as they have spoken here, they will secure a hearing.

We have space but for a few of the facts of this pamphlet; these should be pondered by every man who has property to be taxed, rights to be protected, or children to be saved; and by every citizen who has a stake in the purity and perpetuity of a government of law.

There are 7,779 dram-shops in New York, or one for every 80 of the population, young and old. Of the whole number, just seventy-two pay the decent respect to law to procure a license to sell intoxicating drinks, less than one in one hundred of the shops! But it is not enough to violate one law. It is officially stated that 5,180 of these drinking saloons pursue their traffic on Sunday; and, at a low estimate, the sum of $1,848,330 is expended in them on the Sundays of a year, an amount about equal to that claimed for taxes and charities on account of the pauperism and crime thus created.

But are there not stringent laws against this Sunday tippling? Yes. As late as 1855–57, Laws and Ordinances prohibit it as a misdemeanor, punishable by fine and imprisonment; and twenty-six thousand complaints have already been filed with the District Attorney, and that's all.

Meanwhile look at the fruits of this lawless traffic. It appears that 23,817 of the 27,845 commitments to prison in 1857, were of persons of "Intemperate habits," six per cent. of whom were mere youths and young men between 10 and 30 years; and 21,278 were "foreigners," who make Sunday a day of sport and dissipation.

But another set of statistics demonstrates the immediate connection of crime with the Sunday Liquor Traffic. Taking seventy-six successive Sundays, the criminal records of the Police Department, show that the number of arrest was 9,718; while for the same number of Tuesdays there were but 7,761. Here, then, an increase on Sundays of more than eighteen hundred arrests, or about twenty-five per cent., as compared with other days of the week, is directly traceable to the Sunday dram-shops. These shops were partially closed for a time in the beginning of Mayor Tieman's administration; and then crime on Sundays decreased about one-third.

Have we not found the plague spot? Or do we need to go beyond the record of the fact that seven thousand seven hundred dram-shops, contemn the License Law, and more than five thousand of them, the Sunday Laws, and many of them, the Gambling Laws, to find an adequate cause for the spirit of lawlessness and violence prevailing in our city?

The suggestions of this document as to remedies, are characterized by good sense, and commend themselves at once to public confidence. They are in brief, the change of pay-day from Saturday to Monday or Wednesday; the multiplication of means of innocent popular recreation; the introduction of public fountains, where labouring men may drink without resorting to the dram-shops; the increase of mission churches and other agencies of popular evangelization; the correction and concentration of public sentiment as to Sunday profanations, and the enforcement of the laws against the Sunday Liquor Traffic.

If we do not mistake the tone of public feeling on this subject, the appearance of this document, and the calm but determined attitude of the Committee issuing it, will be welcomed by our citizens generally, with the same cordiality with which the memorial of citizens against the Sunday news crying nuisance was greeted. A happy thing will it be for every good interest amongst us, if the result shall be equally auspicious.

PRESENTMENTS BY GRAND JURIES.

(*Extract from Presentment of Grand Jury at Quarter Sessions, Toronto, O. W., September,* 1859.)

CAUSES OF CRIME, &c.—" On enquiry at the Gaol respecting the cause which has led to so many of the unfortunates therein confined to be sent there, we were informed that in a very large majority it is traceable to the use of spirituous liquors, a statement in which the Toronto officials are borne out by those occupying similar situations throughout Upper Canada. We therefore respectfully request your honor to bring the subject before the Legislature at the next Session of Parliament, requesting them to pass a Prohibitory Liquor Law measure for our country, as we are fully convinced that had we such a law in operation very much of the crime perpetrated in the land would then be put a stop to, and we would not require to increase our gaol accommodation."

(Signed,)   THOMAS NIXON,
Foreman.

The Grand Jury also of the District of St. Francis, C. E., (at Sherbrooke,) in September, 1859, also presented as follows :—"That they have found a large amount of crime in the District, some cases being of a very grave nature ; and judging from the evidence brought before them, they have no hesitation in attributing much of it to the prevalent use of intoxicating liquors, and take pleasure in giving their approval to temperance societies, and other means used for the suppression of intemperance." The Grand Jury also at Niagara, C. W., have presented in a similar manner as the Toronto Grand Jury have so humanely and judiciously done.

There will also be found that in all the Counties of Canada West, presentments have been given against the traffic in intoxicating drinks as the prolific source and cause of crimes, offences, &c. In the County of Perth, Presentments once and again have been made against the traffic and the drinks.

INTOXICATING LIQUORS—PRESERVATION OF THE PUBLIC MORALS.

(CIRCULAR.)

INTOXICATING LIQUORS.

County Buildings, Stratford, 25th June, 1859.

SIR,—The County Council, having in view the reduction of all unnecessary expenditures of monies in the County of Perth, and thereby a lessening of the taxation on the inhabitants, have agreed to submit for your *special consideration* the following paragraphs from public documents laid before them :—(From Presentment of Grand Jury, Mr. George Brown, foreman, Sessions, June, 1859.) " They [the Grand Jurors] have examined the various cases brought before them, " and have to regret, that the major part of them appear to have originated or " been aggravated from the too free use of Intoxicating Liquors."—(From Gaol Surgeon, Dr. Hyde's Report, June, 1860.) " I herewith append a list of Pa- " tients attended by me during the quarter now ended. You will see by the " same, that the great majority of cases requiring my services, have their origin " in the practice of, and indulgence in, the use of Intoxicating Liquors, a custom " by no means decreasing, if we are allowed to take the Criminal Calendar of our " Gaol as a basis for forming an opinion respecting the results of this destroying " beverage."—(From Clerk of Peace, Mr. Linton, June, 1859.) " I have been " Clerk of Peace in this County for about 6½ years, and have directed a good deal " of my attention during that period, to the things in social life, which cause " crimes, petty and larger,—vice, brawls, assaults, irregularities, &c., &c., and " having reference to the many records of crimes passing officially through my

"hands, I have no hesitation in summing up as a whole that *Intoxicating Drinks*
"(with the *traffic* itself, of course,) cause nigh 18 cases out of every twenty
"cases, and comparatively, I consider the County of Perth as rather a model
"County in Western Canada, whether as regards schools, ministers of religion,
"(over 45) roads and ways of business traffic, healthiness and prosperity of the
"people, &c. Yet from March, 1858 to June, 1859, there are, say 850 cases
"reported in the Conviction Lists, and about 760 of these connected with Intox-
"icating Drinks. Many cases also are never heard of, being quashed, &c.,
"and that number does not include Quarter Session and Assize cases. There
"are about 200 places in this County where the Intoxicating Drinks are sold,
"and the population of the County may be about 28,000. There are 14 muni-
"cipalities."

I am instructed to press upon your attention the above subject, with the hope
that all proper means within your power, with your own influence, will be used
for lessening the causes of crime as referable to the custom of the use of "Intoxicating Liquors."

I am, Sir, your most obedient servant,
A. GRANT, <i>Warden.</i></div>

(Copies to be sent to each Justice of the Peace and Reeve, each Constable, to
all the Ministers of religion, to all the Teachers and to each School Section, and
to the Townshi's. Villiage, and Town Clerks, in the County of Perth.) *

REPORT OF THE SPECIAL COMMITTEE ON CIRCULAR FROM WARDEN
OF THE COUNTY OF PERTH.

To THE COUNTY COUNCIL, COUNTY OF SIMCOE:—

The Special Committee to whom was referred the Circular from the Warden of
the County of Perth, on the subject of the traffic *in Intoxicating Liquors, &c.*
BEG TO REPORT on the same subject, and on petition from the inmates of the
County Jail:

That they have given the subject matter of the Circular and Petition, as well
as the whole Liquor question, a careful examination, and have had no hesita-

---

* While the County Council of the County of Perth, were in session
in June, 1859, we suggested to several of its members, and in particular to John
Stinson, and F. Kee, Esqs., J. P., both members of Council, the importance of such a circular letter at the above, being circulated in the County,
and being requested to prepare it, we did so, and it was agreed to, and has been
circulated throughout the County. The County Council agreed to print one
thousand copies of it. Besides, we circulated many hundreds, and it was copied
into various papers, so that its circulation was every where in Canada. We
also sent copies of it to England, Scotland and Ireland. We think that over
50,000 issues of it were made. Copies were sent to each Warden of the other
Counties. The County of Simcoe acted upon it in October. (See papers subjoined.)

In December last, we also submitted a copy of the By-law passed by the
County of Simcoe in October, as to the "preservation of the Public Morals
within the County," and suggested some additional classes. The County Council of Perth, most considerately, humanely, and wisely, passed the By-law with
the additions. It has been printed by them, and an abstract of its provisions will
be seen in *Challenge* No. 23. We have printed an issue of 5,000 of this number,
to go over *all Canada*. The By-law is founded on section 275 of the 22nd Vic.,
c. 99. (Municipal Act of Upper Canada.)

Previous to the above date, we had circulated a copy of the Simcoe By-law in
Challenge No. 20, with a letter addressed to the Warden, A. Grant, Esq., and
Reeves. A similar By-law should be adopted in all the Counties.

[A letter referable to above By-law, will be seen in the *Montreal Witness* of 4th
February, 1860.]

tion in arriving at the conclusion, that it stands forth as the greatest social evil with which any country can be visited, that the baneful effects of the traffic are the same in all countries, corrupting and ruining the young as well as the aged, of both sexes, spreading broadcast desolation, destitution, disease and death, and over and above all this, a very heavy tax upon the community; the fact cannot be controverted, that the expense attendant upon the administration of Criminal Justice in this Province is very materially, indeed, alarmingly increased in furnishing and providing for the unfortunate votaries of intemperance; that the whole traffic is demoralizing in its tendency, and presents a standing and insuperable barrier in the path of both individual and national progress, whether religious, moral, educational, or commercial. At this crisis in our history, your Committee believe that it is the imperative duty of the people of Canada, in whose hands is the destiny of posterity, to place the laws of our country upon so just, healthy and solid a basis, as to secure the greatest amount of happiness, peace and prosperity to the future intelligent, virtuous and loyal millions who may people this noble Province. Your Committee are therefore of opinion, that the Government of this country should make such enactments as would entirely prohibit the traffic in intoxicating liquors, as a beverage, believing as they do, that no government can be justified in deriving its revenue from any system, the tendency of which is to degrade and demoralize the mass of the people; that the suppression of the traffic would be a great benefit to this rapidly growing country, would at once advance the social and moral condition of the people, lessen crime and lawlessness, and lighten taxation.

Entertaining these views, your Committee would recommend your Council to memorialize the Legislature for the enactment of a Prohibitory Liquor Law, to take effect on and after such a date as would afford to all engaged in the liquor business such reasonable time to prepare for such a change in their business as the passage of such a law would render necessary; and beg to submit for the consideration of your Council, the accompanying Draft of Memorial.

All of which is most respectfully submitted,

THOMAS D. McCONKEY,

Committee Room, Barrie, Oct. 20, 1859. *Chairman.*

PETITION *of County Council of County of Simcoe, C. W., to Parliament, for a Prohibitory Liquor Law.*

(EXTRACTS.)

" That your Memorialists have had under their consideration the traffic in intoxicating liquors in this Province, and the consequences resulting therefrom, and can arrive at no other conclusion than that it stands forth as the greatest social evil with which any country can be visited; that the baneful effects of the traffic are the same in every place, vitiating and ruining the young, as well as the aged, of both sexes, spreading broadcast desolation, disease and death, and vastly increasing the burdens of the people by a direct taxation; the expense attending the administration of Criminal Justice in this Province, being also seriously, indeed, alarmingly increased in punishing and providing for the unfortunate votaries of intemperance; that the whole traffic is demoralizing in its tendencies, and presents a standing and insuperable barrier in the path of both individual and national progress, whether religious, moral, educational or commercial.

Your Memorialists are, therefore of opinion that the Government of this country should make such enactments as would entirely prohibit the traffic in intoxicating liquors as a beverage, believing, as they do, that no government can be justified in deriving its revenue from a source so impure, and so pregnant of evil to the great bulk of the people, as is too painfully shown by police reports, prison records, &c., in this country.

Your Memorialists, therefore, humbly and earnestly pray that your Honorable House will be pleased to give the subject of the Liquor Traffic that consideration which its importance demands; and, if deemed politic, pass such a law as

will prohibit the traffic in intoxicating liquor as a beverage, allowing reasonable
time for all engaged in the business, to make such arrangements as the enactment of such a law would necessarily call for.

And, as in duty bound, your Memorialists will ever pray."
Committee Room,
    Barrie, Oct. 20, 1859.

INCENTIVES TO TEMPERANCE FRIENDS.

(From Temperance Advocate, Montreal, Jan. 25, 1855.)

(A.)—TEMPERANCE PAPERS—CIRCULATION.

We desire most earnestly to incite the friends of temperance and prohibition
in Canada West, to the great importance of furthering a more general, as well as
special, circulation of temperance and prohibition papers, especially periodicals;
and that voluntarily and free of any charge to the receiver.

The writer of this has had some experience in the matter of circulation, and
none can tell who have not tried the experiment, of the advantage to the progressing cause of prohibition, in the special circulation, free, which temperance
papers cause.

Let us look over the way, where the new boon of reciprocity causes us to cal-
culate on "perishing gains," (yet profitable every way when beneficially applied), and observe the strenuousness, the "death and life" struggle in the cause
of prohibition, which its friends have pursued, created too, and kept alive by
the New York State Temperance Society, with Mr. Delavan at its head. There
you will see with what earnestness the circulation of temperance and prohibition
papers are promoted. There is no halting,—no "demonstration" without a
practical working result. There is no jealousy or envy, but only to see which
will accomplish most; and the cheering results are now seen in a Maine Law
Legislature (nearly) being elected!

Is it so in Canada? We ask, first, the Grand Division of Canada West, that
question, and then we turn to the "Canadian Temperance League," which
latter certainly has shewn some leaven in obtaining the very valuable help of the
Rev. J. E. Ryerson to lecture in various places; and also in printing, and in
(part gratuitously), distributing temperance tracts and one essay.

But the wide field of Canada West should be embraced in the latter movement,
and no corner of its various settlements should be without some papers being
kindly deposited in the working hands of good men in the moral field, whether
temperance, progressive or religious, for local distribution. Let the Grand
Division and the League look to it, for there is a space to be filled!

How is it to be done? Be up and at it without grumbling, hands in and out
of pocket, and promote the circulation, freely and kindly, all over the land.
How are we to get names of persons? There are friends everywhere, put them
to work, and if there are no friends known, take the local newspapers, and send
to those whose names appear in its columns, trusting not on your plans and
exertions, but leave a Higher and Greater Power to do the rest. Again, through
the thoughtfulness and considerateness of a late Post Master General, the Hon.
M. Cameron, temperance periodicals go free of postage. Thousands of copies of
periodicals can be obtained for a few dollars:—who, therefore, will begin?

We have lately tried to move certain parties on this subject, we trust, to some
extent, successfully. We have applied to a model county, Lambton, through
Mr. Gemmill, the talented editor of the *Lambton Observer*, and we are not
ashamed to repeat our suggestions now, as follows:—"I believe you are aware
" that I have devoted my spare time, also money, to the gratuitous circulation
" extensively of temperance papers, and on a prohibitory law in this county,
" (Perth), and in the county of Bruce, consisting of eleven townships in each;
" and as the people deserve, as well as require some information on the subject of a
" prohibitory liquor law, which at present is before Parliament; and as an ad-
" journment of the House of Assembly has taken place for a short time, would it

" not be well for the friends of the cause *to spread over the land gratuitously* the
" various tracts and periodicals illustrative of the subject. I have so far kept
" various localities in the above counties of Perth and Bruce supplied, and I have
" lately sent through the ten townships of your county of Lambton, various
" papers, namely,—' The Probibitionist,' ' The Tracts by the Canadian League,'
" (3 in number), ' Temperance Tracts for the People ' published at Albany,
" (these are excellent, and above praise), a few of Mr. Case's ' Constitutional
" Rights Vindicated, ' and a good many numbers of ' The Challenge, ' No. 4.
" I have sent to each minister, post master, reeve, treasurer and town clerk,
" some one or all of the above. Permit me to suggest to some of your friends in
" Sarnia, to encourage the circulation of temperance papers in your ten town-
" ships,—in each locality,—and it can be *so easily* done, that it surprises me that
" a system of circulation has not been adopted in each of the forty-two counties
" of Canada West. (I must except the two counties referred to.) "
" I shall also endeavour to induce some friends in 'Essex, Kent, Elgin, and
" Middlesex, to adopt the above plan, and your publishing this letter may help
" in the movement. But the circulation, to have greater effect, should be nearly
" *a gratuitous one,* and we now add *entirely free of charge to the receiver.* So
" may it be !

J. J. E. LINTON.

Stratford, December, 1854.

(B.)—HE IS NO TEMPERANCE MAN WHO WILL NOT SUPPORT WHAT FOLLOWS?

(From the Montreal Temperance Advocate, 15th Dec., 1859.)

STRATFORD, C. W., 9th December, 1859.

DEAR SIR,—It is not often that I trouble you *direct* with any remarks. I do
write, however, continually in the *Temperance* cause, as you know, as the three
papers of this county will show, as well as my own printed papers, the " *Challenge* " and some others, which I scatter gratuitously in this County, and also
east and west by the hundreds and thousands. I have done so for seven years
past. I considered for myself, that, besides *adopting* a principle or plan—say,
namely, the important, very important one of temperance,—there was a duty
incumbent on me, individually, to forward *by every means in my power*, in my
public capacity, and by the Press, an extension of that principle. I could not
rest satisfied with the idea, that as I was (apparently) safe in myself by *refrain-
ing* from any of the fruits of the disastrous traffic in intoxicating drinks, that
therefore I should let the "world wag as it may," *I am safe.* No one is safe,
so long as that most unhallowed and unchristian traffic, worse than unchristian
as it were, that *devilish* traffic, so long as it is the daily and hourly trade of our
noble Province. He is a *selfish* temperance man or woman who will merely
join a temperance cause and then stop. Merely say "yes," and that's all.
I write this, then, preparatory to the beginning of an important season for
action, to call on every man, woman and youngster of the temperance cause,
in-doors and out-of-doors, wherever they are or may be, travelling or at home,
having access to the *influence* of those in a superior station in life, having access
to the labours of their County or City Member of Parliament, in their inter-
course with their Ministers of religion, to devote a portion of their time continually in this good cause, and also to urge its important claims, so as our
Legislative Halls will be presented with Petitions for some enactment whereby
a restraint, an entire restraint if possible, will be put on that system of public
sale by retail in shops, bars, bar-rooms, saloons and groggeries, of those liquids
which already have destroyed so many, and are now destroying and incapacitat-
ing such numbers of our people, besides *causing* the various outrages and crimes
against society, from the case of street drunkenness to the one which leads to
the rope round the neck of the victim on the scaffold.

Ignorance or thoughtlessness may not see, but he is a very *indifferent* person who does not see in the various papers of the Newspaper Press the fruits of the traffic in intoxicating drinks. Without the Newspaper Press, which is so valuable to us, any man or woman who is *not* above making an observation, may see in each of their localities enough to awaken them and convince them, that the traffic is a curse!

I call, therefore, on every one, whether within the ranks of the temperance army or not, or if only merely *approving* of the efforts of temperance men, to consider that there is a duty incumbent on them, for which *some* day, and that a "*great day*," they have to answer for its non-performance according to the "talents" given and bestowed; and it is a duty for all and every one to find out and to know, if they have a talent in keeping and in trust at all. Let each one inclined to a performance, consider himself or herself as though he or she was a President, Worthy Patriarch, or Grand Worthy Patriarch, Secretary or Committee, and therefore individually to work, less or more, but that continually, in the cause of temperance. To be instant in season and out of season. I do not ask any one who may read these words to do anything but what I do myself. *I consider myself Grand Worthy Patriarch of the Grand Division!* That's my idea, and having that idea how can I be idle? I push aside, as in my way, the common lazy and listless expression of thought, namely "that's not my business," it is meddling with what I have nothing to do, let others do it, I have not time, I have no money to spare, I am in business, &c., &c. But the adoption of the idea of duty and support in the temperance cause, makes it a very important personal business, as much so as providing the meat or clothes for the body. I address myself more immediately to professing Christian people. *No one of that class is safe in any duty who acts otherwise.*

I am, yours sincerely,

J. J. E. LINTON.

(C.)—TEMPERANCE.—LAZINESS OF TEMPERANCE FRIENDS.

(*To the Editor of the Christian Advocate.*)

Sir,—It is cheering to observe the movement by the address from the Hamilton Division Sons of Temperance, signed by Mr. Freeman, as published in your truly valuable paper of the 24th instant. Your paper contained also, some time ago, a synopsis of a very excellent lecture on the Prohibition of the traffic in Intoxicating Drinks, by the Rev. Dr. Irvine, of Knox's Church, Hamilton. That lecture should have been widely circulated; and should be, if not yet done.

I write this in reference to the first paragraph (there are others) in the above address, as to Divisions of Sons of Temperance "bestirring themselves" in this great and good cause.

1. There has been, and there exists, a very great and indolent feature in all the temperance associations, viz.: a backwardness to push the cause, in season and out of season, into every corner of the localities where these temperance associations exist. Members, I am afraid, are not charitable enough, think only of *themselves* that as they are apparently *safe*—and they are only apparently— "the de'il tak' the hin'most" as to others. Now, I consider that throughout every place where the Sons of Temperance exist, and where *other* societies exist, their chief endeavour should be *outside of their meeting rooms.*

2. They should endeavour, with all good thinking men, in any station of life, from your talented member, Isaac Buchanan, Esq., M.P.P., to the laborer who does his daily work, and also of every church, to enlist a sound practical feeling and a help towards the temperance cause—a cause the coarse of which I fondly hope is progressing in Canada, and I trust will be yet estimated as one to be considered as far, far beyond the consideration of roads, bridges, sidewalks, or conveniences of life. And how much of the latter engross nearly all our attention in public life. What is the value, the truly honest value, of all the pro-

gressing improvements in your well situated City of Hamilton, when *based* on a state of society as to intoxicating drinks, *which we are ashamed to reveal to the heathen*, for the Christianization and civilization of whom, and for the support of religion, the same parties as likely give largely of their substance? The thing in the eyes of the thinking minds of the unbeliever or the indifferent will appear, as it really is, most hypocritical as before an all-seeing God, an act of hypocrisy and dishonesty as before and amongst ourselves.

3. Riddle and sift the machinery of your society and of your citizens in Hamilton, and beginning from the lowly and outcast (surrounded by the thoughtless and heartless professing Christian) up to the highest merchant in your city, (and there are good men amongst them,) and what will a critical observer see? He will see, he will meet, he will stumble upon an incubus, a parasitical bedevilment, *which no Christian people should show*, but rather what they should be ashamed of. You will find, as in London, C. W., where I have just been, a system engrafted into our society for which the heathens, who worship stocks and stones, (to whom we send out missionaries,) scoff at us, jeer us, and point to it with the finger of scorn, and when a man or woman is seen intoxicated, or even drinking in public, they say, "O, he is a Christian!" That system is the one of *licensing to retail and to sell in set public shops and places intoxicating drinks.*

4. But Hamilton city, the "Queen of the West," as in our prints, is not the only city where the *far worse* than heathenish system above referred to is so predominant, or where the professing Christians tolerate and encourage it. Would to God it was the only city. Look to Ottawa, to Toronto, west to London, to Kingston even, and to Montreal, and to Quebec—the two latter cities, as well as Ottawa, in a particular manner (to those who know anything of the habits of the trade and people)—where the vital and social interests of mankind are sacrificed for money to a system which we are to suppose that devils laugh at and hail as *the very best auxiliary* to increase the population of a certain place.

5. But again, what does the system of the retail trade in intoxicating drinks reveal? It reveals and shows itself, sir, before God and thinking and observing men, as one almost entirely supported and carried on by manufacture, wholesale and by retail, by *Presbyterians, Episcopalians and Roman Catholics!* Let a vigilant investigation be made, and not only the traffic in intoxicating drinks will be found as carried on by members, adherents or those belonging to these churches (such, too, as would not be rejected by either to make up census lists for particular purposes), but the *advertising* of intoxicating liquors in all the papers from Halifax, N. S., to Lake Superior, will be found as being nearly altogether with those of these three churches. I am a Presbyterian of the Free Church, and I hesitated not publicly at the late Synod of our church in Toronto, to bring the accusation before them. My memorial, with accompanying papers, will testify. I did the same to the United Presbyterian Church Synod. Both Synods *declare* against the evil; but still it goes on—"gloriously," as some would say, but sadly, as I state.

6. There is a burden, therefore, put on the members and ministers of other denominations, such as the numerous, vigorous, and vigilant Methodists; also the Baptists and Congregationalists (Independents); for they have to appear in the world and before mankind *as though they were the guilty parties, when they are not.*

I claim *the right* to make the above statements, and the "Conviction List," ending June last, with a number of the *Challenge* endorsed on it, which I sent you lately, may show more than here stated. I have endeavored, as a single Temperance advocate, to wipe away the disgrace of the traffic from the county of Perth, and from Canada, as may be known to you, and at present I have a *prohibitory law* of the retail traffic (according to the Municipal Act of 1858), to be voted on for this town by the people. I send you a copy.* I send also to the

---

* This By-law was negatived by a majority of nigh thirty. The liquor interest was an overmatch for the exertions of all the ministers, and the truly

Hamilton Division several papers. I wish I saw in other places a movement to the same effect—nay, throughout Canada. A blessed time we may well expect it to be, when professedly Christian people will unite to expel from amongst them in their villages, towns and cities, the social sin and evil in their midst, namely, the public retail traffic in intoxicating drinks. And a word for the Hamilton Division—that they endeavour to raise up a feeling for that purpose in Hamilton.

Respectfully, I am, Sir, your most obedient servant,

JOHN J. E. LINTON.

Stratford, C. W., August 26, 1859.

The above letter was published in the *Canada Christian Advocate*, Hamilton, 31st August.

(D.) — EARLY DEVELOPMENT OF THE TEMPERANCE CAUSE IN SCOTLAND, &c.

The Editor of that old and useful paper in this cause, the Montreal *Temperance Advocate*, in the number for the 15th November, suggested that there should be a temperance sermon preached in every pulpit in Canada on the 1st January (being Sunday). We adopted the hint by giving currency to it, in publishing notices in the papers, by quoting the words in the *Advocate*, and also we circulated in *Challenge* No. 22 (copied into several papers), a letter addressed to an esteemed friend, Rev. D. Allan, of North Easthope, on the subject. The following is an extract from that letter:

"*I have known* the day, rather over thirty years ago, in the establishment of the *first* Temperance Society in Great Britain, being at Greenock in Scotland, (our native land) when there was only then *one* minister of religion in Greenock, who would as he did, entertain the subject,—the late and good Mr. Auld,—and I was personally, and know of many others then who were jeered and gibed by minister of religion, because such "a thing" as an organization as to *Temperance* was thought of. Of this I could say more than I desire.—John Dunlop, Esq, (brother of the well known Dr. Dunlop, of Canada,) was the first originator of that society and its President, in September, 1829,—and I had the honor then of being the first Secretary to it. From it, as an example, other organizations in Britain were formed, and have continued and increased. One or two Temperance Societies were previous to that date, but same year, in Ireland, and Dr. Edgar of Belfast, (the same as now on a visit in Canada, I believe) addressed us at our first public meeting. Times have changed as to that subject since;—and I hope the time is now at hand, when every minister of religion, as a duty and to preserve his own "good name" and of far greater importance the name and cause of Him whose servant he is sworn to be, will lay before his people continually and not at sett times (as a duty finished), the great and increasing evil and sin there is in the land, when this Enemy and Foe to Christ's Kingdom, namely intemperance, is so much encouraged by professing Christians, in the devilish system of the open trade by public drinking and use as a beverage, of *Intoxicating Drinks*.

As a public officer of Government, being as you know, Clerk of the Peace of this County, I hesitate not from the facts alone which have been revealed to me

---

Christian people, and others, who voted for it—a deplorable instance of retrogressive Christian and moral civilization! A similar By-law was, however, passed in Wallace, in this County, and, we believe, in Howick, County Huron. But, even, what of all that? The retail shops and places every where else, all around, sell out without restriction, the dangerous liquid, which demoralizes our communities. The law to be effective needs to be a universal one.

as such public officer, during these nigh seven years past (irrespective of half a century's keen and practical observation and remembrance) to denounce the system of the public sale and public drinking, before referred to, as the greatest Enemy and Foe and Satanic means of opposition, to the successful promulgation and reception to Christ's Kingdom in our land, which exists.

I hope therefore, that you and the other ministers of religion in this County— and I hope it will be universal in Canada,—will consider of the suggestion made by the Editor of the *Temperance Advocate* as above quoted.

I am, Rev'd and dear Sir,

Yours sincerely,

5th Dec., 1859.   J. J. E. LINTON."

SAMPLE OF ADVERTISEMENTS OF SALES OF LIQUORS.

As our readers know, the sample from the newspapers published, of these advertisements, might be increased indefinitely, as their number, in every shape, sad to state, is "legion." We insert the following, cut from the *Hamilton Spectator* of the 5th January. We ask our readers also to direct their attention to the article in these pages, titled "Adulterations of Liquors," referable to the whole subject, and especially to the letter appended, of Dr. Hiram Cox, of Cincinnati, of date Oct. 3rd, 1859, inserted in the *Montreal Witness*, of the 4th February :—

"WINES, &c., for New Year's, at GEORGE DARTNELL'S.—Brandy, pale and dark ; Rum, Old London Dock ; Gin, Old Tom and Hollands ; Whiskey, Scotch, Irish, Bourbon, Monongahela, Old Rye, Toddy and Canadian. Port, Sherry, Champagne, Burgundy, Claret, Moselle, Liqueurs, &c. London and Dublin Porter, East India Pale Ale, Canadian Pale and Strong Ales, and Extra Stout ! ! This Establishment is the only one in Hamilton *exclusively* engaged in the Whole-sale and Retail Wine and Spirit business."

"A CARD.—The subscriber has on sale a choice lot of old and fine Sherry, Madeira and Champagne Wines. Old Brandy, vintage 1840, in cases, and in hhds. 1852–'54. Old Irish and Scotch Malt Whiskey, and Canadian of best makers. Also, a varied assortment of Spices, Sauces, Pickles, Fruits, Coffees, Teas and Sugars, which he will sell for cash only, at lower prices than the same quality of goods can be bought at in any house in Canada. Those who are aware of the benefit of cash purchases would confer a favor on the subscriber by telling their friends how much is saved by the cash system.—R. BENNER, Agent and Commission Merchant, corner of King and John streets."

ADULTERATIONS OF LIQUORS.*

DR. HIRAM COX'S LETTER.

From the Montreal Witness, of February 4th, 1860.

"ASTOUNDING DISCLOSURES. — Many charges have been made against dealers in intoxicating liquors, as engaging in vile and dangerous adulterations. The Legislature of Ohio, in March 1855, directed Dr. H. Cox, a distinguished chemist of Cincinnati, to make a thorough examination of such liquors as are in the market. The following letter from Dr. Cox to James Black, Esq., of Lancaster, Pa., gives the result of his investigations. We advise every man who is in the use of intoxicating liquors to read it carefully, and then *think before he drinks.*

---

* See previous article herein on " Adulterated Liquors."

Can a man walk on hot coals, and his feet not be burned?—can he take poison into his stomach, and not be injured?"

"CINCINNATI, OHIO, Oct. 3, 1859.

"JAMES BLACK, ESQ.—Dear Sir,—Yours of the 29th Sept., dated Lancaster, Pa., is now before me. Although not personally acquainted, I take great pleasure in contributing my mite, in any and every possible mode, where the object is the bettering of the human family. I have had similar letters, with similar requests, from every point of the compass—from the extreme north, south, east and west—to all of which I have cheerfully responded; believing, although the labor has been considerable, that it would tell in after years in the longevity and health of thousands who would otherwise fill a premature grave, and would contribute to the happiness and comfort of thousands of mothers and children, who are and have been, unfortunately, connected with the unfortunate slaves of intemperance. I rejoice to know that my exposures of the *villainous* liquors with which the markets east and west are glutted, have had a salutary moral influence in almost every region of our happy Union. I have letters in my possession from ministers of the gospel, from New Orleans, from Nashville, Tenn., from Florida, from New York, from Boston, from Richmond, Va., Alexandria, Norfolk, Washington city, Baltimore, Philadelphia, Pa., from Toronto, and from Hamilton, (Canada,) and from all of our Eastern States, congratulating and encouraging me to continue my exposures—that they were causing men to think and stand aghast, more than anything that they could do or say on the subject of Temperance. The same effect has been produced in this community. One gentleman tapped me on the shoulder some little time past, and remarked at the same time, 'Doctor, I rejoice to see you take the stand that you do on the subject of poisonous liquors. I can lay my hands on more than thirty of our best citizens, gentlemen who were tippling and tippling from a dozen to twenty times a day, and who were bidding fair to fill a drunkard's grave, who have stopped short, and do not, and pledge themselves that they never will, drink any more, for fear they may get hold of some of the miserable adulterations that Dr. C is holding up to public view. Thank God!'

"Chemists from various colleges have written to me, stating that they analyzed numerous samples of the various alcoholic liquors in our markets, and found the same pernicious developments which I had at various times indicated in articles which I had written from time to time; one of which you will find at page 123 of the *Crusader*, which accompanies this letter.* Another evidence that the exposures which I have been making have had a salutary moral effect is, that there has not been one-fourth as much liquor sold yearly since as was previously; and another is, that a number of large liquor establishments have closed, their proprietors ruining many of their fellow-citizens who had become their sureties. A number of distilleries have closed in this vicinity; they have, as it is familiarly called, 'burst their boilers.' One year previous to these break-ups, one of our largest distillers and liquor merchants in the city said to me, 'Dr. Cox, your articles on the adulterations of liquors have taken more trade from Cincinnati, and more money—at least $100,000 per month—since they have been put in circulation. For God's sake, stop them, sir!—you will break us up. I have been to New York, and since to Boston, to Rochester, to Canada West, and have just returned; and wherever I stopped there was nothing talked of but the poisoned liquors of Cincinnati and Dr. Cox's exposures. For God's sake, I say again, stop it!'

Although the liquors are villainous in the extreme, there are *other* large cities equally as culpable. For example; a gentleman of our city, a druggist, that he might have pure liquor as a medical article, and that kind for purity, &c., that he could recommend to his customers, went to New York and purchased two half-pipes of splendid "Seignette Brandy," one *pale*, the other *dark*. When

---

* The "Crusader," we have omitted to state, is a noble and lion-hearted Temperance paper, published at Cincinnati (Ohio,) by Messrs. Cary & Moffatt.

passing one day, he called me in to see his *"beautiful pure* brandy," just from New York! I stopped, looked at it, smelt it, but, before tasting it, happened to have some blue litmus paper in my pocket, I introduced a small piece—it came out red as scarlet! I then called for a polished spatula, put it into a tumbler containing, perhaps, half a gill, and waited on it fifteen minutes, at the expiration of which, the liquor was as black as ink. The spatula corroded, and when dried, a thick coating of rust, which, when wiped off, left a copper coat almost as thick as if it had been plated. I charged him on the spot, under the penalty of the law, not to sell a drop of it; took samples of it to my office, and the following is the result of the analysis, viz. :

1st sample (*dark*), 55 per cent. alcoholic spirits by volume, and 41 per cent. by weight; specific gravity 0,945. The tests indicate Sulphuric Acid, Nitric Acid, Nitric Ether, Prussic Acid, Guinea Pepper, and an abundance of Fusil Oil. Base—common whiskey, not one drop of wine.

2nd sample (*pale*), 54 per cent. alcoholic spirits by volume, 40 per cent. by weight; specific gravity 0,955. This article has the same adulterations as the first, but in greater abundance, with the addition of Cathuc. Remark—Most villainous connections.

As a matter of course, these articles of liquor could not be sold without a violation of the liquor law, consequently I condemned them. They were purchased on four month's time. The purchaser immediately notified the New York merchant of the character and quality of the goods, and directed him to send for them; but, instead of sending for them, he waited till the notes became due, and brought suit in our Court of Common Pleas. I analyzed the liquors in the presence of court and jury, shewed them satisfactorily that they were the pernicious, poisonous and villainous liquors which I had represented them to be, and the defendant gained his case triumphantly; and Mr. New York merchant vanished before I could get a State's warrant, or he would now be learning an honest mode of making a living at one of our State Institutions in Columbus. I was appointed to the office of Chemical Inspector on the 19th day of March, 1855—since then, I have made upwards of 600 inspections of stores, and lots of liquors of every variety, and positively assert that 90 per cent. of all that I have analyzed were adulterated with the most pernicious and poisonous ingredients. The business of inspecting against the will of men who are only governed by motives of cupidity, I have found an up-hill business. I have had more *lawing*, more squabbling and quarrelling, with unprincipled things, bearing the shape and form of men, made after God's image, since I have been engaged in the capacity of Inspector, than I had during half a century before. You may think I have heard it thunder some; well, so I have. I am 66 years old, but in all my recollection I have not heard *thunder* that had the same effect on my nervous system, nor anything else to affect my sympathetic nerves so much as the sad effects of imbibing the miserable concoctions sold in our markets under the character of healthy beverage, with which *Cock-tails, Brandy-smashes, Mint-juleps, &c., &c.,* are concocted, and which sent young men, all under 30 years old, and all sons of men of our most respectable citizens, to a premature grave, during the winter previous to my appointment; some of whom had not been drinking three months! Not only young men, but many old men of our city, who were not considered drunkards, died during the same winter, the horrid death of the drunkard with the *Delirium Tremens!* These facts induced me to accept the unthankful appointment. Since the appointment, I have, as Physician to the Probate Court, examined upwards of 400 insane cases, two-thirds of which number became insane from drinking the poisonous liquors sold at the groggeries and taverns of our city and country. Many of them were boys from 19 to 20 years of age, some of whom were laboring under a hereditary taint; and perhaps in many of them, the mental derangement would never have been developed, had they not drank of these poisonous decoctions. One boy, 17 years of age, the principal support of a widowed mother and a little sister, was induced on the Fourth of July, 1855, to drink some *beer,* and from *beer* to the horrible *rot-gut whiskey,* kept in the low groggeries of our city. They all got drunk, and the boy referred to became hopelessly and incurably insane, and is yet in the Insane

Asylum at Dayton. In examining the case for the purpose of getting all the antecedents with it, I learned that the grandfather of the boy died insane. I think the probability is altogether in favor of the idea that the insanity would never have been developed in this case, had not these poisonous admixtures acted as a powerful excitant cause. I called at a grocery store one day, where liquor also is kept. A couple of Irishmen came in while I was there, and called for some whiskey; and the first drank, and the moment he drank the tears flowed freely, while he at the same time caught his breath like one suffocated or strangling. When he could speak, he said to his companion: "Och, Michael, but this is warming to the stomach!" Michael drank, and went through like contortions, with the remark, "Would'nt it be foine in a cowld frhosty morning?"

After they had drank, I asked the landlord to pour me out a little in a tumbler, in which I dipped a slip of litmus paper, which was no sooner wet than it put on a scarlet hue. I went to my office, got my instruments and examined it. I found it had 17 per cent. alcoholic spirits by weight, when it should have had 40 per cent. to be proof, and the difference in per centrge made up by Sulphuric Acid, Red Pepper, Pellitory, Costic, Potassa and Brucine, one of the salts of Nucis Vomiæ, commonly called Nux Vomica. One pint of such liquor would kill the strongest man. I had the manufacturer indicted, but by such villainy he has become wealthy, and I never have, owing to some defect in the law, been able to bring that case to a final issue.

Yours, respectfully,   HIRAM COX, M. D.

---

* As we were revising the proof sheets, a friend in Sarnia sent us the Sarnia *Observer* (published by J. H. Gemmil, Esq.) of 17th February, wherein is a long and valuable report on "Inspection of Liquors," by Mr. L. G. Miller, of Detroit, Inspector of Liquors and Wines for Wayne County, Michigan—and *his* evidence is only corroborative of the extensive "adulterations" of every kind, "innocent, deadly, and spuriously fine," used in liquors. Mr. Miller is a practical chemist, having had experience in Europe and America. He states: "In 382 cases of inspection of whiskey, he only discovered two cases of pure."——"So far as regards the article of brandy, he was not able to find, after inspection, a single drop of pure French brandy."——"High wines have been imported into France *from the United States*, and exported therefrom, after undergoing a certain process, to the United States and other countries, under the false name of pure French brandy."——"In 164 samples of gin, found but 29 samples genuine." ——"In 82 samples of Jamaica rum, he found *only nine* samples of genuine and pure rum."——"Of the Port wine, *a* genuine article is seldom sold * * * By analysis, he found among all his inspections *only eight* samples of genuine and pure."——"Of Champagne wines, there is to be found in this or any other country but a small portion genuine."——"It is a well established fact, that there is more Champagne, or its imitation, consumed in New York city in one month, than it is possible to manufacture from the grapes raised in all the vineyards of the province of Champagne for one season." The above testimony is valuable. It only surprises us that after such statements as Mr. Miller's and Dr. Cox's, and Mr. Delevan's, and the others, are known, that *men and professing Christians* sell them, (yet *such men* manufacture them!) and we wonder that the class of tipplers and drinkers who drink in public, are not "wiser in their generation," and *abandon* these liquors and find *purer articles!*

BOOKS.—We omitted to state that there is a good authority to refer to in the "Temperance Cyclopedia," by Rev. W. Reid, of Edinburgh —enlarged edition—to be obtained at the *Witness* Office, Montreal; and the Rev. R. D. Wadsworth, of Hamilton, C. W., is preparing to publish "The Teetotaller's Vade Mecum," 500 pp. 12mo, price $1; and a valuable addition will also be in the book of Amasa McCoy, Esq., of Albany, N. Y., "The History of the Temperance Cause," &c., which we learn will soon be published.

www.ingramcontent.com/pod-product-compliance
Lightning Source LLC
Chambersburg PA
CBHW021553270326
41931CB00009B/1197